Scientific Challenges
To Evolutionary Theory

How These Challenges Affect Religion

T0321524

Scientific Challenges To Evolutionary Theory

How These Challenges Affect Religion

Jay Schabacker

Jayschab@aol.com
www.CreationClass.org

ELM HILL

A Division of
HarperCollins Christian Publishing

www.elmhillbooks.com

Scientific Challenges to Evolutionary Theory
How These Challenges Affect Religion

Published in Nashville, Tennessee, by Elm Hill, an imprint of Thomas Nelson. Elm Hill and Thomas Nelson are registered trademarks of HarperCollins Christian Publishing, Inc.

Elm Hill titles may be purchased in bulk for educational, business, fund-raising, or sales promotional use. For information, please e-mail SpecialMarkets@ ThomasNelson.com.

Scripture quotations marked KJV are from the King James Version. Public domain.

Scripture quotations marked NIV are from the Holy Bible, New International Version˚, NIV˚. Copyright © 1973, 1978, 1984, 2011 by Biblica, Inc.˚ Used by permission of Zondervan. All rights reserved worldwide. www.Zondervan.com. The "NIV" and "New International Version" are trademarks registered in the United States Patent and Trademark Office by Biblica, Inc.˚

Library of Congress Cataloging-in-Publication Data

Library of Congress Control Number: 2019931461

Pre-Launch ISBN: 978-0-310103783

ISBN 978-0-310103790 (Paperback)
ISBN 978-0-310103806 (Hardbound)
ISBN 978-0-310103813 (eBook)

DEDICATION

This book is dedicated to the late
Dr. Henry M. Morris (1918–2006),
widely recognized as the founder of the modern
Creation Science movement.

"The need, therefore, for a worldwide revival of the doctrine of real creation and a personal creator God is great. God's urgent message to Job and his contemporaries is more vital now than ever before."[1]

---

[1] Dr. Henry M. Morris, *The Remarkable Record of Job* (Green Forest, AR: Master Books, 1999/2000), 94.

Also

A quote by mayor of Chicago, Rahm Emanuel, August 2018

"I know the power of what faith and family can do. Our kids need that structure. I am asking… that we don't shy away from a full discussion about the importance of family and faith helping to develop and nurture character, self-respect, a value system, and a moral compass that allows kids to know good from bad and right from wrong."

ACKNOWLEDGEMENTS

A fter a long journey of love and challenges that now have burst forth into this book, I want to thank those who helped me make this possible.

So many scientists (more than can be named) have put forth their valued testimony, and I give my thanks to them all. Of course, a special thanks in this book's dedication is given to Dr. Henry M. Morris (1918-2006), considered the founder of the modern creation science movement.

By God's grace, this effort came to fruition, and accordingly, I give thanks to the helpful and supportive members of Lexington Presbyterian Church (South Carolina) and the First Presbyterian Church of Columbia, South Carolina.

As the project moved along, many contributed with help and assistance: Linda Lee and Tammie Bairen gave much needed editorial help, and JoAnn Craten gave website support. Barbara Weller of the National Center for Life and Liberty was always there for advice when needed.

Two organizations, mentioned in the book, should be acknowledged for their efforts to positive change. Two names stand out:

David Schmus of the Christian Educators Association International (CEAI) for their pioneering works in the public schools.

Dr. John West of the Discovery Institute for their timely initiation of the Academic Freedom Petition.

I thank Elm Hill Books, a division of HarperCollins Christian Publishing for all those who tirelessly worked on the project.

Last but not least, my continued thanks go out to my loving wife, Nancy Schabacker, who was patient throughout all my toils and gave advice and encouragement when needed.

Jay Schabacker
Lexington, South Carolina

CONTENTS

Is there an answer to the violence and the shooting?

"Scientific Challenges To Evolutionary Theory"

To save our country by saving our kids.

PREFACE

We are in the "Age of Discovery."

A s an engineer, I like to research and discover, and that's where I get in trouble—because then I write about it. But I'm passionate about it, so it gets lengthy. Here, I will try some short Cliffs Notes.

1. I discovered that the number of scientists who believe in the Creation is a very great number. This didn't jibe with what the general public is told 'that scientists cannot be Creationists.' After my Mount St. Helens experience, I decided to research what the scientists had to say about the Biblical Creation—and hence this book, "Scientific Challenges To Evolutionary Theory."[2]

---

[2] Jay Schabacker, "The Scientists Speak," Creation in Classrooms, http://www.creation class.org/.

Lahar Flowing Down Mount St. Helens, March 21, 1982
USGS Photo by Tom Casadevall

2. <u>I discovered that it is all about a giant battle between two opposing belief systems:</u>,

–the belief that there is no supreme being, but instead a naturalistic worldview, Uniformitarianism, and chance for evolution taking place over billions of years for impossible events to take place;

–the belief in Catastrophism (think "global flood"), wherein we understand a miracle-performing God is forever creating and sustaining in ways we have to admit we don't fully understand.

3. <u>I discovered that school kids are taught evolution and evolution only in their school science classes.</u>
Throughout this book, you'll see a spattering of opinions, such as:

"The chance of our being here is so slim that it is enough to leave us goggle-eyed with terror—until in the next moment we realize that we are indeed here and explode with gratitude for our very existence. This can really be the only proper and logical response to

it all, to marvel and rejoice and rest in the genuinely unfathomable miracle of our being."

– Eric Metaxas, *Miracles*[3]

"Scientists may be able to show mathematically consistent ways in which the existence of these somethings could lead to other somethings. But what are the odds that something can come from absolutely nothing? There is not a chance."

– R.C. Sproul, *Not a Chance*[4]

"I, at any rate, am convinced that He is not playing with dice."

– Albert Einstein

"Miracles are not a contradiction of nature. They are only in contradiction of what we know of nature."

–Saint Augustine

4. I discovered that there are more than 500 accounts of a global flood from all over the world, handed down from generation to generation, and eventually written down.

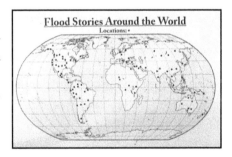

5. I discovered that scores of people have discovered the remains of Noah's Ark on top of Mount Ararat. Just one story is from 1985 when US Air Force General George Havens saw the re-creation of the Ark that

---

3   Excerpts from *Miracles: What They Are, Why They Happen, and How They Can Change Your Life* by Eric Metaxas, copyright © 2014 by Metaxas Media, LLC. Used by permission of Dutton, an imprint of Penguin Publishing Group, a division of Penguin Random House LLC. All rights reserved.

4   R.C. Sproul and Keith Mathison, *Not a Chance: God, Science, and the Revolt Against Reason* (Ada Township, MI: Baker Books, 2014). Used by permission. All rights reserved.

George Hagopian described (pix below): "We've seen that. We have photos of that. Our pilots have photographed that very object. It looks just like that. It is on a ledge. In fact, I was shown two slides of this object at Fort Leavenworth in a presentation for people assigned to Turkey."

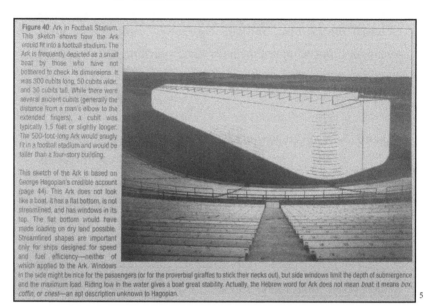

Figure 40. Ark in Football Stadium. This sketch shows how the Ark would fit into a football stadium. The Ark is frequently depicted as a small boat by those who have not bothered to check its dimensions. It was 300 cubits long, 50 cubits wide, and 30 cubits tall. While there were several ancient cubits (generally the distance from a man's elbow to the extended fingers), a cubit was typically 1.5 feet or slightly longer. The 500-foot-long Ark would snugly fit in a football stadium and would be taller than a four-story building.

This sketch of the Ark is based on George Hagopian's credible account (page 44). This Ark does not look like a boat, it has a flat bottom, is not streamlined, and has windows in its top. The flat bottom would have made loading on dry land possible. Streamlined shapes are important only for ships designed for speed and fuel efficiency—neither of which applied to the Ark. Windows in the side might be nice for the passengers (or for the proverbial giraffes to stick their necks out), but side windows limit the depth of submergence and the maximum load. Riding low in the water gives a boat great stability. Actually, the Hebrew word for Ark does not mean *boat*; it means *box, coffin*, or *chest*—an apt description unknown to Hagopian.

6. In addition, I discovered that ancient peoples of the 'Near East' wrote extensively detailed accounts (on rock) of incidents and happenings also detailed in the Holy Bible. Here is just one such item.

7. I discovered that a huge body of information explaining the Creation Model and refuting the Evolution Model has been

Clay tablet; New Babylonian. Chronicle for years 605–594 BC © The Trustees of the British Museum

---

[5] Walt Brown, *In the Beginning: Compelling Evidence for Creation and the Flood*, 8th edition (Center for Scientific Creation, 2008), Figure 40.

building and is gaining strength yearly. This information needs to be made available to all of us.

Evolutionist Gerald Hawkins in his book *Mindsteps to the Cosmos*, states, "I do not wish to get involved with the evolution 'argument'. Did it take place slowly over the aeons, or did it move forward in a spectacular jump—could a hopeful monster appear on the scene by mutation and find a niche? Was there a sudden change in the brain caused by a quirk, or was the modern mind a slow and steady 3 million years in the gestation?"[6]

Though Hawkins did not want to get involved in the 'argument', we must!

As enumerated later in this book, the social consequences of the belief in evolution are numerous and negative! Just to name a few: *our animal-like behavior, meaninglessness, good overtaken by evil, communism, relativism, secular humanism, divorce, racism, and abortion. So much more we hear in the daily news!*

> *"The lesson of history is clear: when Christian belief is strong, the crime rate falls; when Christian belief weakens, the crime rate climbs. Widespread Christian belief creates a shared social ethic that acts as a restraint on the dark side of human nature."*[7]

Also, a recent quote by City of Chicago mayor, Rahm Emanuel, August 2018:

> **"I know the power of what faith and family can do. Our kids need that structure. I am asking ... that we don't shy away from a full discussion about the importance of family and faith helping to develop and nurture character, self-respect, a value**

---

6   Gerald Hawkins, *Mindsteps to the Cosmos*, 1st edition (New York: HarperCollins, 1983), 6.

7   Charles Colson with Nancy R. Pearcey, *A Dance with Deception* (Nashville: W Publishing Group, 2004), 190.

system, and a moral compass that allows kids to know good from bad and right from wrong."

I have also learned that the evolutionists never give up, and they are well organized. One case in point is Antonio Gramsci, a leader in  the Italian Communist Party in 1939, who wrote, "A cultural hegemony was necessary. It would be accomplished via a 'long march through the institutions' to take over and transform schools, colleges, magazines, newspapers, theaters, cinemas, and art. It was necessary to control opinion-forming centers to change the prevailing culture, but primarily to eliminate Christian influences."[8]

8. I have also discovered that the evolutionists fib a lot:

"Fourteen Years and Still Counting!"

School boards, even now, fourteen years after prominent atheist and evolutionist Dr. Richard Dawkins made his original statement on December 3, 2004, in an interview with journalist Bill Moyers that **"There is massive evidence for the theory of evolution,"** are still parroting the same statement today. Now, Glenn Branch, deputy director for the National Center for Science Education, Oakland, CA, said, in December 2017: **"What's taught about evolution in California's public schools is supported by overwhelming amounts of evidence from multiple areas of science."**[9]

When you read on in the book, you will come in contact with a number of evolutionist fakes and frauds, including: Ernst Haeckel's evolution embryo fraud, Piltdown Man, Nebraska Man, Java Man, Neanderthal Man, Lucy the hominid, Orce Man, and archaeoraptor fake dinosaur bird, horse evolution fraud, brontosaurus, flipperpithecus.

---

[8] Gazegorz Gorny and Janusz Rosikon, *Fatima Mysteries: Mary's Message to the Modern Age* (San Francisco: Ignatius Press, 2017).

[9] Guy McCarthy, "Science and religion: Can they coexist in the same classroom? Should they," *The Union Democrat*, December 7, 2017, https://www.uniondemocrat.com/localnews/5822862-151/science-and-religion-can-they-coexist-in-the.

"Scientific Challenges to Evolutionary Religion"

Moving ahead to what the scientists say, the engineer in me caused to be spilled a major amount of ink in the book dedicated to the 'argument'— the scientific differences between the <u>Creation Model</u> and the <u>Evolution Model</u>. In this preface, I relate a short part of Dr. Duane Gish's article, *Summary, Scientific Evidence for Creation*[10], as follows:

<u>Formation of Earth's Geological Features</u>

1. <u>Creation Model:</u> The earth's geological features appear to have been fashioned largely by rapid, catastrophic processes that affected the earth on a global and regional scale (catastrophism).
2. <u>Evolution Model:</u> The earth's geological features were fashioned largely by slow, gradual processes, with infrequent catastrophic events restricted to a local scale (uniformitarianism).

<u>Life on Earth—Thousands of Years or Billions of Years?</u>

1. <u>Creation Model:</u> Life was suddenly created.
2. <u>Evolution Model:</u> Life emerged from nonlife by naturalistic processes.

9. <u>I discovered that an evolutionary group of scientists believe that life on earth cannot be more than 100,000 – 200,000 years old, 'Ref. Please see pages 55-58.'</u>

<u>Use of Radiometric and Other Dating to Get Accurate Results of Age</u>

1. <u>Creation Model:</u> The inception of the earth and of living kinds may have been relatively recent.

---

[10] Duane Gish, PhD, "Summary of Scientific Evidence for Creation (Part I & II)," Institute for Creation Series, May 1, 1981. Used by permission. https://www.icr.org/article/summary-scientific-evidence-for-creation/.

2. Evolution Model: The inception of the earth and then of life must have occurred several billion years ago.

Emergence of Plants and Animals: What the Fossil Record Shows

1. Creation Model: All present living kinds of animals and plants have remained fixed since Creation, other than extinctions, and genetic variations in originally created kinds have only occurred within narrow limits.
2. Evolution Model: All present kinds emerged from simpler earlier kinds so that single-celled organisms evolved into invertebrates, then vertebrates, then amphibians, then reptiles, then animals, then primates, including man.

Mutations: Required by Evolution—Are They Good or Bad?

1. Creation Model: Mutation and natural selection are insufficient to have brought about any emergence of present living kinds from a simple primordial organism.
2. Evolution Model: Mutation and natural selection have brought

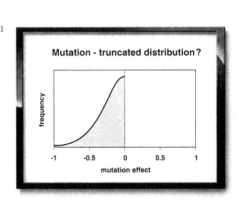

Figure 3b.
Population geneticists know that essentially all mutations are deleterious, and that mutations having positive effects on fitness are so rare as to be excluded from such distribution diagrams. This creates major problems for evolutionary theory. But this picture is still too optimistic.

---

[11] Dr. J. C. Sanford, *Genetic Entropy and the Mystery of the Genome Classroom Edition*, 3rd edition (Massachusetts: Feed My Sheep Foundation, Inc., 2008), Figure 3b, 27. Used by permission.

about the emergence of present complex kinds from a simple primordial organism.

Man and Apes

1. Creation Model: Man and apes have a separate ancestry.
2. Evolution Model: Man and apes emerged from a common ancestor.

Emergence of the Universe and the Solar System

1. Creation Model: The universe and the solar system were suddenly created.
2. Evolution Model: The universe and the solar system emerged by naturalistic processes.

The scientists have tons of detailed sound evidence for Creation and against Evolution, so please consider reading more in later chapters of this essay.

10. I discovered that evolution is a Religion—Not science

Ardent Darwinian atheist Michael Ruse has acknowledged that evolution is their religion. Here is what he said, and there are many more who say the same thing.

"Evolution is promoted by its practitioners as more than mere science. Evolution is promulgated as an ideology, a secular religion—a full-fledged alternative to Christianity, with meaning and morality. I am an ardent evolutionist and an ex-Christian, but I must admit that in this one complaint—and Mr. Gish (Duane T. Gish the Creation Scientist) is but one of many to make it—the literalists are absolutely right. Evolution is a

religion. This was true of evolution in the beginning, and it is true of evolution today."[12]

Also, Sir Julian Huxley, the primary architect of modern neo-Darwinism, called **evolution a 'religion without revolution."**

The Takeaway Here

1. The Christian cause is being hurt by the teaching of evolution (and only evolution) in the public schools. As Will Provine says—"Belief in modern evolution makes atheists out of people."
2. The "Establishment Clause" should prohibit the **nonscientific religion of evolution** as much as it prohibits the **scientific religion of Creation** in our public schools.
3. **A powerful legal case may be made for the allowance of the teaching of the scientific aspects of the Creation Model beside the scientific aspects of the Evolution Model in our public schools.**

11. I discovered that Democrats are urging Socialists to become teachers because they can't win in a "fair fight"

So What Is the Action Plan?

Many firmly believe that more emphasis on the Christian worldview most likely would bring about improved results socially for our population. (Again, consider the sorrowful situation in the evening news every night!) Therefore, they believe that public schools allowing the covering of Creation would be a positive thing.

---

[12] Michael Ruse, "Is Darwinism a Religion?" *Huffington Post*, last modified September 20, 2011, https://www.huffingtonpost.com/michael-ruse/is-darwinism-a-religion_b_904828.html.

Poll Results on the Desire in Teaching as the Percent of the Population

1.	Teach Darwin's Theory of Evolution only	21%
2.	Teach Evolution plus **scientific evidence against it**	**69%**
3.	Not sure	<u>10%</u>
		100%

Some courageous proponents of Creationism in public schools have put forth legislation often entitled "Academic Freedom Acts." There have been only two victories:

1. A Louisiana "Science Education Act" was passed in 2008.
2. A Tennessee act was passed in 2011 to "protect a teacher from discipline for teaching scientific subjects in an objective manner."

But the overall results were depressing. From a report of the National Center for Science Education (NCSE), which is pro-Evolution, in the period 2008–2015, from sixteen states, "Academic Freedom Acts" were <u>brought before a committee or the legislature fifty one times and were denied 96 percent</u> of those times. Louisiana and Tennessee made up the two victories—4 percent.

"Thank you everyone for signing the petition."

Yes, the battle for legislation is being lost because the atheist minority is more forceful, more aggressive, and louder. They are well-organized and often put forth petitions to the school boards and state legislators that win them the victory. One petition put together by Eduardo Pazos, using petition model *Change.org*, was titled "Stop FL anti-evolution bill (SB 1854)." It was submitted to the Florida State House with 284 signers in July 2011. The last statement by Eduardo Pazos was: "The bill is dead. Thank you everyone for signing the petition."

It is understandable if the courageous legislators who led the fight with the previous unsuccessful bills are now "burned out" and *discouraged*. **But we are in the majority, and we are in the right—so let's take heart and get to work.**

Yes, it's now time for the silent majority to finally come forward and lead the fight—with "grassroots" campaigns and a series of informational presentations and petitions as needed. Led by church pastors and members, Creation scientist groups, legislators, and concerned citizens could make an important difference if:

1. We all read about the subject and start the conversation toward Creation teaching allowed in the public schools.
2. We gave our views to the school boards and legislators who are the decision-makers.
3. We initiate and put forth needed petitions in support of needed legislation.

In addition, or as an alternative to success with the public schools, it is suggested church pastors take steps to create their own church schools or promote other local Christian schools to their members. Also, concerned families can start their own home schooling program for their children.

12. I discovered that an active 'Academic Freedom Petition' is promoting the teaching of Creation in public schools

And, yes, we now have our own petition! It's called the 'Academic Freedom Petition.' Please consider signing it: https://freescience.today/petition/

To Save Our Country by Saving Our Kids

INTRODUCTION

Lahar Flowing Down Mount St. Helens, March 21, 1982
USGS Photo by Tom Casadevall

We were traveling the Lewis and Clark Trail and came upon a destination we always wished to visit—Mount St. Helens. The eruption on May 18, 1980, of that mountain in the state of **Washington was something historical—especially for scientists who try to explain our earth's** recent history through catastrophes. Not actually scientists but Christians with a seeking mind, my wife and I found the site exciting. At the end of the tour, I approached the salesperson and asked if they had any books with a Christian view of the catastrophism shown by Mount St.

Helens; the reply, to my chagrin, was, "**I'm sorry, sir, but we only carry books by scientists.**"

I was taken aback to say the least, hence the idea to write this book that started with the goal of researching what advanced level scientists had to say about Biblical Creation.

It was a lot!

Who Are the Scientists?

Eric Metaxas in his book *Miracles* provides us with a short introduction:

"**There are many leading scientists who unapologetically believe in God and miracles,** who see no conflict between a life simultaneously dedicated both to faith and scientific inquiry.

"This alone should be dispositive. For example, Francis Collins, who appeared on the cover of *Time* for his work heading the Human Genome Project, and who now is the director of the National Institutes of Health—and who for his fame as a scientist was on President Obama's 2008 transition team. Indeed, in his book *The Language of God*, he explains how it was science itself that led him to embrace his Christian faith. Another top scientist, Cambridge's Sir John Polkinghorne, after being recognized as one of the top quantum physicists of the twentieth century—and being elected to the Royal Society—was ordained as an Anglican priest and now regularly writes and speaks on the compatibility of science and faith. And, finally, Dr. William D. Phillips, who won the Nobel Prize in physics in 1997, has spoken widely about how his dedication to science and God are not merely compatible but conjoined and logically inextricable from one another. **The list of contemporary men and women of science who believe in the God of the Bible and in miracles is virtually endless.**

"We are only surprised by this—if we are—because our culture has so forcefully promoted the idea that faith and science are at odds, but the ironic and virtually unknown reality is that modern science itself was essentially invented by people of the Christian faith. That's because they believed in a God who created a universe of staggeringly magnificent order, one that could be understood rationally, and one that was therefore worth trying to understand. Many of them believed scientific work was a way of glorifying God, because it revealed the spectacular order and manifold genius of God's creation.

"Isaac Newton himself was a serious Christian, and Galileo, who because of his battles with the Catholic Church is often thought of as a scientist at odds with Christian faith, was in fact a committed Christian. To add just two from the many others we might name, John Clerk Maxwell and Michael Faraday were both men of deep Christian faith, whose breadth of scientific genius cannot be overstated, and whose faith explicitly underpinned their zeal to understand the laws governing the universe."[13]

Creation Ministry Organizations

How about in our present day?

In our present times, there are many excellent organizations committed to Biblical Creation and committed to getting the information out to us. Here are five such large organizations you might want to contact at the outset of our discussion:

Institute for Creation Research (ICR), Founded 1970
Home office: Dallas, Texas
Of interest: The ICR Discovery Center for Science and Earth History
www.icr.org, 800-337-0375

Creation Ministries International (CMI), Founded 1977
Home office: Australia; also Atlanta, Georgia

---

[13]   Metaxas, *Miracles*, 23–24.

Of interest: The CMI Journal of Creation, Creation Magazine, Creation Daily, and movie Alien Intrusion
www.creation.com, 800-616-1264

Discovery Institute (DI), Founded 1990
Home office: Seattle, WA, also Alexandria, VA and Frisco, TX
Of interest: With an Intelligent Design emphasis—The Center for Science and Culture, Evolution News & Views, Discovery News, and the 'Academic Freedom Petition'
www.discovery.org and www.discovery.org/id, 206-292-0401

Answers in Genesis (AIG), Founded 1994
Home office: Petersburg, Kentucky
Of interest: Creation Museum, Ark Encounter, and the Answers Magazine
www.answersingenesis.org, 859-727-2222

Geoscience Research Institute, Founded 1958, Seventh Day Adventist Church
Home office: Loma Linda, CA
www.grisda.org, 909-558-4548

Further, there are approximately 123 Creationist organizations, large and small, just in the United States of America—in the various states, and this listing is shown in an Appendix G. [14]

---

[14] Creation Ministries International, "Creationist organizations in the United States of America," accessed November 8, 2018, https://creation.com/creationist-organizations-in-the-usa.

Then, how about the number of individual scientists with PhDs?

Recent Believers in Biblical Creation who Possess a Doctorate in a Science-Related Field

It is a long list, in Appendix A, of "Some scientists alive today* who accept the biblical account of creation."[15]

*Note: Some of those listed may be recently deceased, and some names may have been inadvertently omitted. **The list includes 223 names.***

Names are taken from the following:

"Some scientists alive today* who accept the biblical account of creation"

Please see also for more lists:

- "Creation & Earth History Museum, Creation Scientists"[16]
- Also of interest: There is a new list of more than 1,000 doctoral scientists names, world-wide, who shares their doubts about Darwinian Evolution. Please go to: www.dissentfromdarwin.org.[17]

Recent Believers in Evolution Who Possess a Doctorate in a Science-Related Field

The few names I have found are taken from a number of sources, including the following, below. But the list has been extremely hard to pin down

---

[15] Creation Ministries International, "Some scientists alive today* who accept the biblical account of creation," accessed November 8, 2018, https://creation.com/scientists-alive-today-who-accept-the-biblical-account-of-creation.

[16] Creation & Earth, "Creation Scientists," accessed November 8, 2018, http://creationsd.org/about/creation-scientists/.

[17] Evolution News, "Skepticism About Darwinian Evolution Grows as 1,000+ Scientists Share Their Doubts," accessed February 6, 2019, https://evolutionnews.org/2019/02/skeptism-about-darwinian-evolution-grows-as-1000-scientists-share-their-doubts/.

when looking for active and published PhDs in appropriate science-related fields. I don't include a list here, as it is subject to review.

1. "On Evolution—Love It Or Hate It"[18]
2. "A Who's Who of evolutionists"[19]
3. "List of popular science books on evolution" - Wikipedia[20]
4. "Famous Evolutionary Biologists/List of Top Evolutionary Biologists"[21]

Note: It is a fact that 'Darwin Doubters' do get expelled from US universities if their views become known. So it is probably true that PhDs at universities gladly sign up on the evolution side if they want to retain their tenure. At the university level, professors are warned: "Tow the line on evolution—or else."

Ben Stein, in his popular 2008 documentary, "Expelled: No Intelligence Allowed," brought to light what he calls a dogmatic commitment to Darwinism at US universities. He stated, "It is not just the scientists who are in on it. The media is in on it, the courts, the educational system, everyone is after them."[22]

[18] Simon Cleveland, PhD, "On Evolution—Love It Or Hate It," Goodreads, June 13, 2009, https://www.goodreads.com/list/show/2228.On_Evolution_Love_It_Or_Hate_It.

[19] Don Batten, "A Who's Who of evolutionists," Creation International Ministries, December 1997, https://creation.com/a-whos-who-of-evolutionists.

[20] Wikipedia, "List of popular science books on evolution," last modified March 2, 2018, https://en.wikipedia.org/wiki/List_of_popular_science_books_on_evolution.

[21] Ranker, "List of Famous Evolutionary Biologists," accessed November 8, 2018, https://www.ranker.com/list/notable-evolutionary-biologist_s)/reference?ref=search.

[22] Cornelia Dean, "Scientists Feel Miscast in Film on Life's Origin," *The New York Times*, September 27, 2007, A1.

HERE IS SOME GENERAL INFORMATION

Creation to Darwinism – A Little History

Across the centuries, the account of the Biblical Genesis has been accepted in Jewish, Christian, and Muslim societies as the true story of human beginnings. Then, in the mid-nineteenth century, Europeans and Americans alike were stunned by a proposal that men and women had not been created suddenly in their mature form by a supreme heavenly power. Instead, they had evolved gradually over eons of time from simpler forms of animal life through a process of mutation and natural selection by which varieties of animals that were well suited to survival as their environments changed would prosper, and those not well suited would die off. Therefore, humans were not unique beings entirely separate from other animals. They were part of a complex pattern of linked life forms. The detailed version of that proposal appeared in the book, *The Origin of Species* (1859) by Charles Darwin, an English naturalist, and the scheme became known as the Theory of Evolution.

Darwin's theory was not greeted with great joy in his day, nor is it universally accepted today. In the late nineteenth century, the theory was condemned from most pulpits; and the general public did not welcome the unattractive likelihood that their close biological relatives might have been apes and monkeys and that more distant ancestors could have been chickens, toads, and garden slugs. However, a massive accumulation of empirical evidence over the decades gradually convinced scientists of the theory's worth, so that today much of biological science as taught in schools is founded on an updated version of the Theory of Evolution called neo-Darwinism.[23]

"I myself am convinced that the theory of evolution, especially the extent to which it's been applied, will be one of the great jokes in the history books of the future. Posterity will marvel that so very flimsy and dubious a hypothesis could be accepted with the incredible credulity that it has."

(Malcolm Muggeridge—world famous journalist and philosopher—Pascal Lectures, University of Waterloo, Ontario, Canada).12. The Evolution Juggernaut— Evolution in Our Culture and Our Education System

---

The Evolution Juggernaut—Evolution in Our Culture and Our Education System

We just viewed the scientist situation, but recently we realize that we are up against something more sinister—the fact being that evolution is in our culture, and our education system is impacted in a catastrophic way! Now that I have gotten a taste of it, I have read much to learn more, and probably, so have you. Here are three items:

1. *"Evolution is taught as undisputed fact in public schools across the nation. Each day millions of children learn that life arose naturalistically over millions of years of slow, gradual processes.*

---

[23] R. Murray Thomas, *God in the Classroom: Religion and America's Public Schools* (Lanham, MD: R&L Education, 2008), 58.

They learn that we're all related through one common ancestor. Students are rarely taught the major problems with evolutionary ideas (and trust me, there's plenty of baseless speculation!) and they certainly aren't given any alternatives."[24]

2. And, says Denyse O'Leary, "*The textbook publishing industry depends on a simple set of facts:*

   - *Parents are required by law to present their children to the local public school system unless they can afford other legally acceptable arrangements.*
   - *Homeowners and businesses are required to fund the public system.*
   - *The system needs textbooks.*
   - *Textbook authors, usually successful teachers, are well rewarded.*

   Thus, the opportunities for soft corruption (stale, dated content that lingers year after year) are vast and inevitable. Some such stuff is doubtless defended by pressure groups, anxious to retain a discredited icon that supports their cause."[25]

3. Also, on the cult of "science," Philip Bell writes: "*Thankfully, there are occasional voices of reason to be heard above the clamour. In May 2016, the influential American 'Journal of Religion and Public Life,' First Things, carried an article appropriately entitled 'Scientific Regress.' Referring to what the author called the '*Cult of Science,*' he wrote, "the cult is related to the phenomenon described*

---

[24] David Rives, "How Evolution Infiltrated Schools and Universities," David Rives Ministries, November 20, 2017, www.davidrivesministries.org/how-evolution-infiltrated-schools-and-universities-david-rives/.

[25] David Klinghoffer, "But *Why* Do Biology Textbooks Retain Discredited Evolutionary Icons?" Evolution News & Science Today, September 14, 2017, https://evolutionnews.org/2017/09/but-why-do-biology-textbooks-retain-discredited-icons/.

*as '**scientism**'; both have a tendency to treat the body of scientific knowledge as a holy book or an a-religious revelation that offers simple and decisive resolutions to deep questions.... Some of the Cult's leaders like to play dress-up as scientists—Bill Nye and Neil deGrasse Tyson are two particularly prominent examples—but hardly any of them have contributed any research results of note. Rather, Cult leadership trends heavily in the direction of educators, popularizers, and journalists."[26]*

The "Long March through the Institutions" Plan

But it gets even more sinister than that! We must step back in time to 1939 (perhaps we should go further back than that, but let's choose 1939). Antonio Gramsci, leader of the Italian Communist Party, was an advocate of cultural Marxism and the author of the "long march through the institutions" plan to take over and transform schools, colleges, magazines, newspapers, theaters cinemas, and art— primarily to eliminate Christian influences.

As Grzegorz Gorny and Janusz Rosikon wrote in *Fatima Mysteries*, "*Gramsci was perturbed as to why the proletariat in Europe did not support Bolshevism. He concluded that the working masses had a false consciousness, as it had been infected by Christianity, the most serious obstacle to worldwide Communism. According to him, the working masses were unable to recognize their real class interests, as their souls had imbibed ideas from the Gospels. Hence the assumption of power would not solve the problem, as politicians were not in control of human souls. Therefore a cultural hegemony was necessary. It would be accomplished via a* "long march through the institutions"*

---

[26] Philip Bell, "The Unstoppable evolutionary juggernaut?" Creation Ministries International, November 7, 2017, https://creation.com/unstoppable-evolutionary-juggernaut.

to take over and transform schools, colleges, magazines, newspapers, theaters, cinemas, and art. It was necessary to control opinion-forming centers to change the prevailing culture, but primarily to eliminate Christian influences." [27]

And Now the Latest from the Socialists

Radio host Michael Knowles said on August 25, 2018, "**that Democratic Socialists are urging Socialists to become teachers because they can't win in a 'fair fight.'**"

A pamphlet by the Young Democratic Socialists of America (YDSA), in conjunction with the Democratic Socialist Labor Commission, outlines a push for socialists to 'take jobs as teachers' as a way to move teachers' unions 'in a more militant and democratic direction.'

Campus Reform reported that the YDSA's 11-page pamphlet notes teachers are able to use their relationships with students to discuss 'campaigns around police brutality, immigration rights, and environmental justice.' (See full article in Appendix F)

"There was little doubt that the star intellectual turn of last week's British Association for the Advancement of Science meeting in Salford was Dr. John Durant, a youthful lecturer from University College Swansea. Giving the Darwin lecture to one of the biggest audiences of the week, Durant put forward an audacious theory— that Darwin's evolutionary explanation of the origins of man has been transformed into a modern myth, to the detriment of science and social progress.... Durant concludes that the secular myths of evolution have had 'a damaging effect on scientific research,' leading to 'distortion, to needless controversy, and to the gross misuse of science.'" [28]

—*Dr. John Durant (University College Swansea, Wales)*

---

27 Gorny and Rosikon, *Fatima Mysteries*, 193.

28 Dr. John Durant, "How Evolution became a scientific myth," New Scientist 87, no. 2 (September 11, 1980): 765.

Fourteen Years and Still Counting!

Even now, fourteen years after prominent atheist and evolutionist Dr. Richard Dawkins made his original statement on December 3, 2004, in an interview with journalist Bill Moyers that, **"There is massive evidence for the theory of evolution,"** evolutionists are still parroting the same statement today. [29]

Now, Glenn Branch, deputy director for the National Center for Science Education, Oakland, CA, said, in December 2017: **"What's taught about evolution in California's public schools is supported by overwhelming amounts of evidence from multiple areas of science."** [30]

Summary of Scientific Evidence for Creation

Dr. Duane Gish, the late past vice president of the Institute for Creation Research, provides this excellent scientific presentation of the differences between the **"creation model"** and the **"evolution model."** (See http://www.icr.org/article/summary-scientific-evidence-for-creation/). Dr. Gish covers the seven major areas (I–VII) of dispute between the creationists and the evolutionists, and we will let his comments introduce the seven areas as we present them in the following pages.

I am going to present Dr. Gish's comments in a different order because I want to begin with the Global Flood (VI). I do this for two reasons:

---

[29] PBS, "NOW Transcript," December 3, 2004, http://www.pbs.org/now/transcript/transcript349_full.html.

[30] McCarthy, "Science and religion."

1. The Global Flood is key to the adjudication of the two major arguments:

   a. *Catastrophism,* or the formation of the geology of the earth by rapid catastrophic processes such as the Global Flood and a Young Earth (as presented by the Creationists)

   b. *Uniformitarianism,* or the formation of the Earth's features by slow, gradual processes, taking billions of years (as presented by the evolutionists)

2. Corroboration of events in the Holy Bible has been systematically and scientifically shown in numerous cases and, most importantly, in cases that attest to the actuality of the Global Flood on earth.

Non-Biblical Evidence that Corroborates People and Events in the Holy Bible

"Let the debate continue, but let the evidence be admitted. Ever since scientific archaeology started a century and a half ago, the consistent pattern has been this: the hard evidence from the ground has borne out the biblical record again and again—and again. The Bible has nothing to fear from the spade."[31]

Indeed, **what was chronicled in the Bible was also chronicled and corroborated by many other writings, on tablets of stone, from dynasties and locations nearby.** Here, following, are just two shown, while in an Appendix B, there are eight.

---

[31] Paul L. Maier, "Biblical Archaeology: Factual Evidence to Support the Historicity of the Bible," Christian Research Institute, March 30, 2009, www.equip.org/article/biblical-archaeology-factual-evidence-to-support-the-historicity-of-the-bible/.

Gilgamesh Epic
Akkadian
Early 2nd millennium BC
Ref. Genesis 6-9

"In reality, it was Utnapishtim's flood, told in the eleventh tablet. The council of gods decided to **flood the whole earth** to destroy mankind. But Ea, the god who made man, warned Utnapishtim from Shuruppak, a city on the banks of the Euphrates, that he should build an enormous boat....

"Flood Tablet" (British Museum)
Photo: BabelStone via Wikimedia Commons

Utnapishtim sealed his ark with pitch, took ... his family members [and all kinds of vertebrate animals] plus some other humans. Shamash the sun god showered down loaves of bread and rained down wheat. Then the flood came ... [Later], the ark lodged on Mt. Nisir (or Nimush), almost 500 km (300 miles) from Mt Ararat."[32]

Merneptah Stele
Egyptian
13th century BC

The discovery of the Israel Stele is very important in the study of Biblical archaeology. It is the oldest evidence of Israel in the land of Canaan in ancient times outside the Bible. The text on the stone reads: *Canaan is plundered with every evil way. Ashkelon is conquered and*

"Merneptah Stele"
(Egyptian Museum)
Photo: Webscribe via
Wikimedia Commons

---

[32] Jonathan Sarfati, "Noah's Flood and the Gilgamesh Epic," Creation Ministries International, September 12-17, 2006, https://creation.com/noahs-flood-and-the-gilgamesh-epic.

brought away captive, Gezer seized, Yanoam made nonexistent; Israel is wasted, bare of seed." – Merneptah Stele[33]

Flood Stories from All over the World!

The question of the "flood" is of major importance because of the variation between "models":

1. The evolution model of *Uniformitarianism* asserts no global flood.
2. The creation model of *Catastrophism* asserts a global flood.

The numerous flood myths or **deluge myths** are, taken collectively, myths of a great flood. These accounts depict global flooding, usually sent by a deity or deities, to destroy civilization as an act of divine retribution. Flood stories are common across a wide range of cultures, extending back into the Bronze Age and Neolithic prehistory.[34]

You see, per Biblical account, after the worldwide flood, eight people remained as eyewitnesses; then, after the Tower of Babel, their descendants dispersed all over the world and told the stories handed down from generation to generation. These stories, over 500 of them, were written down in all corners of our present world. In summary:[35]

1. West Asia and Europe
   1.1 Ancient Near East

---

[33] Bible History, "The Israel Stela (Merneptah Stele)," accessed November 8, 2018, http://www.bible-history.com/archaeology/egypt/2-israel-stela-bb.html.

[34] Mark Isaak, "Flood Stories from Around the World," The Talk Origins Archive, last modified September 2, 2002, http://www.talkorigins.org/faqs/flood-myths.html.

[35] Wikipedia, "List of flood myths," last modified November 5, 2018, https://en.wikipedia.org/wiki/List_of_flood_myths.

1.1.1 Sumerian

1.1.2 Mesopotamia (Epic of Gilgamesh)

1.1.3 Abrahamic religions (Noah's flood)

1.2 Classical Antiquity

1.3 Medieval Europe

1.3.1 Irish

1.3.2 Welsh

1.3.3 Norse

1.4 Modern era folklore

1.4.1 Finnish

2. Africa

3. Asia-Pacific

3.1 China

3.1.1 Yu the Great

3.1.2 Great Flood

3.2 India

3.2.1 Puluga

3.2.2 Manu and Matsya

3.3 Korea

3.4 Malaysia

3.5 Philippines

3.5.1 Igorot

3.6 Tai-Kadai people

3.6.1 Temuan

3.6.2 Orang Seletar

4. Oceania

4.1 Polynesia and Hawaii

5. Americas

5.1 North America

5.1.1 Hopi

5.1.2 Inuit

5.2 Mesoamerica

5.3 South America

5.3.1 Canari

5.3.2 Inca

5.3.3 Mapuche

5.3.4 Muisca

5.3.5 Tupi

The figure below shows the locations where some of those flood stories were found. For more, see, "Flood Stories from Around the World." But beware, this report of flood stories numbers 127 pages!

Flood Stories Around the World

Locations: •

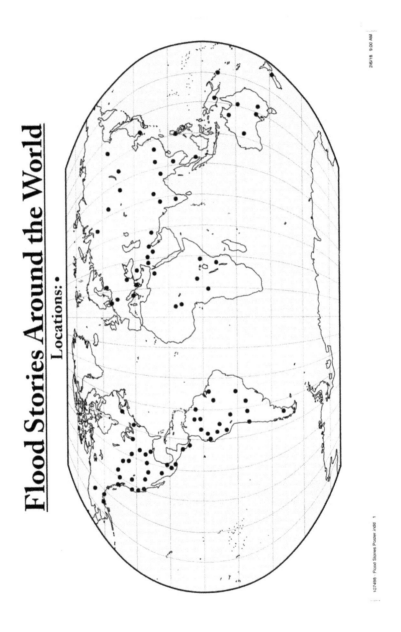

Eyewitness Accounts of Noah's Ark on Mount Ararat

Yes, there was a worldwide flood and the real Ark of Noah. As we will find, later in this book, scientists will tell us what we can understand because of the world-wide flood. Is there anything else? Yes! We have found the Ark! Those hundreds who live around the Mount Ararat area can tell you all about it. The US government and the Air Force can tell you all about it—but apparently they want to keep it quiet and have labeled the photos "Top Secret." There are at least seven eyewitness accounts of Noah's Ark on Mount Ararat:

1. 1800s – Jacob Chuchian
2. 1908 – George Hagopian
3. 1916 – Czar Nicholas II
4. 1943 – Sergeant Ed Davis
5. 1945 – Air Force Corporal Lester Walton
6. 1974 – Navy Lieutenant JG Al Ahappell
7. 1985 – US Air Force General Ralph E. Havens

In 1985, when the US Air Force General George Havens saw the re-creation of the Ark that George Hagopian described (see picture), he said, **"We've seen that. We have photos of that. Our pilots have photographed that very object. It looks just like that. It is on a ledge. In fact, I was shown two slides of the object at Fort Leavenworth in a presentation for people assigned to Turkey."**[36]

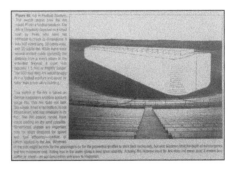

---

[36] Vance Nelson, *Untold Secrets of Planet Earth: Flood Fossils*, First Revised Edition (Alberta, Canada: Untold Secrets of Planet Earth Publishing Company Inc., 2014), 32-50.

The seven eyewitness accounts are detailed in this book in Appendix C.

The New (After the Flood) World

Dr. Henry M. Morris, in his book, *The Genesis Record* states:

The world had not been annihilated by the Flood, but it was drastically changed. As the apostle Peter says, "The world that then was, being overflowed with water, perished" (II Peter 3:6). When they left the Ark that had preserved them through that year of God's awful wrath, Noah and his family truly disembarked into a new world. The Ark had provided the bridge seemingly fragile and easily demolished from the old cosmos through the terrible Cataclysm to the present cosmos, "the heavens and the earth which are now" (II Peter 3:7).[37]

With the global flood a certainty, let's get further into the issues—and **let the scientists and others speak to us about the Biblical Creation.**

"Chance" vs. "Miracles"

A comment or two on the evolutionary model seems appropriate. Chance and a lot of time seem to be needed for this model. Note: the renowned late Dr. Robert Charles (R. C.) Sproul penned more than seventy books— among them was his recent, *Not a Chance*. The next five items are from that book.

1. Nobel Laureate George Wald said, **"One only has to wait: time itself performs the miracles." "Given so much time,"**

---

[37] Dr. Henry M. Morris, *The Genesis Record: A Scientific and Devotional Commentary on the Book of Beginnings* (Grand Rapids: Baker Book House, 1976), 211.

continued Wald, "the 'impossible' becomes possible, the possible probable, and the probable virtually certain." Here is magic with a vengeance. Not only does the impossible become possible; it reaches the acme of certainty—with time serving as the Grand Master Magician. In a world where a miracle-working God is deemed as anachronism, he is replaced by an even greater miracle worker: time or chance. [38]

2. Chance as a calculation of probability factors certainly "works" in a bridge game or dice bet, which we have seen. As an aid to mathematical models, chance surely works. As an aid to grasping real states of affairs, it fails—and fails miserably. **Pragmatism may well be served by attributing causal power to chance, but truth and subsequently science are negotiated away in the process.**[39]

3. **Chance as a real force is a myth**. It has no basis in reality and no place in scientific inquiry. For science and philosophy to continue the advance in knowledge, chance must be demythologized once and for all.[40] (Sproul, page 203)

4. Charles Darwin (*The Origin of Species*) "himself once wrote to J. D. Hooker, '**I cannot look at the universe as the result of a blind chance….**'" [41]

Here is the conclusion: Why is there something rather than nothing? "In the beginning God created the heavens and earth" (Gen. 1:1, NIV). This is the answer revealed by the Creator himself. Those who deny God have suggested other alternative answers, but as we have seen, they reduce to self-contradictory nonsense. Gravity is not nothing. Space is not nothing. A multiverse is not nothing. **Scientists may be able to show**

---

[38] Sproul and Mathison, *Not a Chance*, 28.

[39] Sproul and Mathison, *Not a Chance*, 50.

[40] Sproul and Mathison, *Not a Chance*, 203.

[41] Sproul and Mathison, *Not a Chance*, 45.

mathematically consistent ways in which the existence of any of these somethings could lead to other somethings. But what are the odds that something can come from absolutely nothing? There is not a chance."[42]

The Issue and the Argument: The Gut Issue

Evolutionist Gerald Hawkins, in his book *Mindsteps to the Cosmos,* states, "I do not wish to get involved in the evolution argument: Did it take place slowly over the aeons, or did it move forward in a spectacular jump—could a hopeful monster appear on the scene by mutation and find a niche? Was there a sudden change in the brain caused by a quirk, or was the modern mind a slow and steady 3 million years in the gestation?" [43]

Though Hawkins did not want to get involved in the argument, we must!

As Dr. Henry Morris states in his book *Science and the Bible*, "The creation-evolution question is certainly the most important area of apparent conflict between the Bible and science. It is a great mistake for Christians to compromise on this issue or, perhaps even worse, to ignore it. Although our nation was founded on creationist principles and all the early schools in our country taught Creation, Evolution has now become the dominant philosophy and for several generations has been taught as fact in practically all our schools.... Evolutionary assumptions also dominate the news media and all our public institutions. It has probably contributed more to the prevalent secularistic and materialistic philosophy of the world today than any other influence. It seems obvious that an issue that is so vitally significant ought to be seriously studied by all thinking men and women." [44]

So, to understand Creation, the Bible must be viewed seriously.

---

[42] Sproul and Mathison, *Not a Chance*, 223.

[43] Hawkins, *Mindsteps to the Cosmos*, 6.

[44] Dr. Henry Morris, *Science and the Bible* (Chicago: Moody Publishers, 1986), 37.

A July 28, 2012 message from the Institute for Creation Research, stated (in part),

> *"The Bible clearly states that God created the 'heaven, and the earth, the sea and all that is in them is' (Exodus 20:11) out of nothing. 'Things which are seen were not made of things which do appear' (Hebrews 11:3). The first verse of the Bible, 'In the beginning God created the heaven and the earth,' could be paraphrased: God called into existence the space-mass-time (i.e., heavens-earth-beginning) universe. Evidently before creation, nothing now intrinsic to the universe existed at all.*
>
> *While this teaching is clear, not hard to understand, it is hard to believe. Such 'ex nihilo' (i.e., out of nothing) creation is so foreign to our experience that it can only be comprehended as God reveals it to us. We are taught that His creative work was finished at the sixth day of the creation week (Genesis 2:1-4). With the exception of certain of the miracles of Christ on Earth, such creation has not occurred since, and we have difficulty believing it could happen, so foreign is it to our experience."* [45]

Enter the Bible: "Science in the Bible"

Dr. Henry Morris, in his book, *Science and the Bible*, penned,

> *"One of the most amazing evidences of the divine inspiration of the Bible is its scientific accuracy. There are many unexpected truths that have lain hidden within its pages for thousands of years, only to be recognized and appreciated in recent times. These principles are not expressed in modern technical jargon, of course, but nevertheless are presented accurately and beautifully, indicating*

---

[45] John D. Morris, PhD, "Our Understanding of Creation," Institute for Creation Research, July 28, 2012, https://www.icr.org/article/6844/.

remarkable understanding of nature by these ancient authors far in advance of their 'discovery' by modern scientists." [46]

The figure below, "Science Confirms the Bible,"[47] is taken from a number of locations, variously, *Scientific Facts in the Bible* and *Evidence Bible: Way of the Master.*

[46] Morris, *Science and the Bible*, 11.

[47] Living Waters Publications, "Scripture Confirms the Bible," Used by permission. http://store.livingwaters.com/science-confirms-the-bible.html.

Science Confirms the Bible

(Bear in mind that the Bible was written 2,000–3,000 years ago)

THE BIBLE	SCIENCE NOW	SCIENCE THEN
The earth is a sphere (Isaiah 40:22).	The earth is a sphere	The earth was a flat disk.
Incalculable number of stars (Jeremiah 33:22).	Incalculable number of stars	Only 1,100 stars.
Free float of earth in space (Job 26:7).	Free float of earth in space.	Earth sat on a large animal.
Creation made of invisible elements (Hebrews 11:3).	Creation made of invisible elements (atoms).	Science was mostly ignorant on the subject.
Each star is different (1 Corinthians 15:41).	Each star is different.	All stars were the same.
Light moves (Job 38:19,20).	Light moves.	Light was fixed in place.
Air has weight (Job 28:25).	Air has weight.	Air was weightless.
Winds blow in cyclones (Ecclesiastes 1:6).	Winds blow in cyclones.	Winds blew straight.
Blood is the source of life and health (Leviticus 17:11).	Blood is the source of life and health.	Sick people must be bled.
Ocean floor contains deep valleys and mountains (2 Samuel 22:16; Jonah 2:6).	Ocean floor contains deep valleys and mountains.	The ocean floor was flat.
Ocean contains springs (Job 38:16).	Ocean contains springs.	Ocean fed only by rivers and rain.
When dealing with disease, hands should be washed under running water (Leviticus 15:13).	When dealing with disease, hands should be washed under running water.	Hands washed in still water.

The Creation Model – *Miracles*

Author, Ronald H. Nash wrote in "Are Miracles Believable?"

"Miracles are essential to the historic Christian faith. If Jesus Christ was not God incarnate, and if Jesus did not rise bodily from the grave, then the Christian faith as we know it from history and the Scriptures would not—could not—be true (see Rom 10:9–10). It is, then, easy to see why enemies of the Christian faith direct many of their attacks against these two miracles: Christ's incarnation and resurrection in particular and the possibility of miracles in general.

What one believes about the possibility of miracles comes from that person's **worldview**. On the question of miracles, the critical worldview distinction is between naturalism and supernaturalism. For a naturalist, the universe is analogous to a closed box. Everything that happens inside the box is caused by, or is explicable in terms of, other things that exist within the box. *Nothing* (including God) exists outside the box; therefore, nothing outside the box we call the universe or nature can have any causal effect within the box. To quote the famous naturalist Carl Sagan, the cosmos is all that is or ever has been or ever will be. The major reason, then, why naturalists do not believe in miracles is because their worldview prevents them from believing.

If a naturalist suddenly begins to consider the possibility that miracles are really possible, he has begun to move away from naturalism and toward a different worldview. **Any person with a naturalistic worldview could not consistently believe in miracles.** No arguments on behalf of the miraculous can possibly succeed with such a person. The proper way to address the unbelief of such a person is to begin by challenging his naturalism.

The worldview of Christian theism affirms the existence of

a personal God who transcends nature, who exists "outside the box." Christian supernaturalism denies the eternity of nature. God created the world freely and *ex nihilo* (out of nothing). The universe is contingent in the sense that it would not have begun to exist without God's creative act, and it could not continue to exist without God's sustaining activity. **The very laws of the cosmos that naturalists believe make miracles impossible were created by this God. Indeed, one of naturalism's major problems is explaining how mindless forces could give rise to minds, knowledge, and sound reasoning.** [48]

Eric Metaxas has a lot to say in his book, *Miracles*. The next several items are from that book:

"Whether one believes in miracles or the miraculous has mostly to do with the presuppositions one brings to the subject. What presuppositions do we have in asking whether there might be something beyond the natural world? All of us have presuppositions about the nature of things, about whether something can be beyond what we experience with our five senses. Sometimes our presuppositions are the result of our education, but they are just as often determined by, or at least partly the result of, our upbringing and the culture in which we were raised."[49]

The more science learns, the clearer it is that, although we are here, we shouldn't be. Once we begin considering the details of it all, the towering odds against our existence begin to be a bit unsettling. When we come to see the superlatively extreme precariousness of our existence, and begin to understand how by any accounting, we ought not to exist, what are we to think or feel? Our existence seems to be not merely a virtually impossible

---

[48] Ronald H. Nash, "Are Miracles Believable?" in *The Apologetics Study Bible*, (Nashville: Holman Bible Publishers, 2007), 79.

[49] Metaxas, *Miracles*, 5.

miracle but the most outrageous miracle conceivable, one that makes previously amazing miracles seem like almost nothing.

It's as if someone logically convinced you that the odds of being able to take your next few breaths were infinitesimally small. If we really believed it, we would begin to breath cautiously, perhaps even timidly and tentatively, expecting our next intake of breath to yield no oxygen. **The slimness of our being here is so slim that it's enough to leave us goggle-eyed with terror—until in the next moment we realize we are indeed here and explode with gratitude for our very existence. This really can be the only proper and logical response to it all, to marvel and rejoice and rest in the genuinely unfathomable miracle of our being.**[50]

"I, at any rate, am convinced that He is not playing with dice."
– Albert Einstein

But there are two questions that must be answered.

The first is: Why haven't we heard any of this before? Of course a few people have heard some of it before, perhaps in a sermon by a hip, especially knowledgeable, apologetics-focused pastor. But the majority of people have not. Why haven't they? Mainly because what the public comes to learn always lags far behind what science learns, whether via the media or via textbooks in the classroom. So if in recent years new information has been discovered, it doesn't mean that this information will be disseminated to the public immediately. Even most scientists lag far behind on much of this new information and still cling to outdated concepts and theories. Each scientist focuses on his or her field and can hardly be expected to be up on the latest cosmological theories

---

[50] Metaxas, *Miracles,* 54.

any more than a family doctor can be expected to know what is happening on the cutting edge of research on every disease. It's simply not possible. **Finally, many scientists hold so strongly to materialistic assumptions that they are predisposed against these ideas and simply may not take them seriously enough to look further into them.** The more time passes, however, the more evidence emerges supporting the fine-tuning theory, so the general scientific consensus grows broader each day, making it more difficult to justify dissent. Of course, this does not mean some do not try.

This leads to our second question. What are we to make of what have been called the "anything but that" theories, which rather desperately try to find ways around the mounting evidence for—and implications of—a finely tuned universe? The most popular at present is the so-called multi-universe—or "multiverse"—theory, which postulates the existence of an infinity of other universes "that we cannot perceive." According to this almost comically clever idea, if there exists an infinity of other universes—and this is an infinitely big "if"—one of them must of course *by chance* possess all the variables perfectly right for everything to exist just as it does in fact exist—and would you be very surprised to learn that we just happen to exist in that one universe? How lucky for us. Of course, there is no scientific evidence for this theory, unless perhaps we simply "cannot perceive" the evidence. Of this multiverse theory, eminent physicist Sir John Polkinghorne has said: "Let us recognize these speculations for what they are. They are not physics, but in the strictest sense, metaphysics. There is no purely scientific reason to believe in an ensemble of universes." Philosopher Richard Swinburne put it less diplomatically: "To postulate a trillion-trillion other universes, rather than one God, in order to explain the orderliness of our universe, seems the height of irrationality."

So having answered these two questions and holding only

to what science is able to tell us at the beginning of the twenty-first century, it seems impossible to avoid logically concluding that the existence of our universe is a miracle, one of impossible proportions. The more we know, the clearer it is that we should not be here to think about being here. We are a distinct mathematical impossibility. Do we simply shrug at this and move on, or dare we consider its implications? To simply say *'It is what it is'* or to prestidigitate the escape hatch of an infinity of universes is to ignore the sharp point of the assembled facts.[51]

The essential meaning of miracles, then, is to point us to the God behind the miracles. In the New Testament we see that Jesus performed miracles precisely to prove that he was who he said he was. And in the Old Testament, God performed signs and wonders to attest to who he was. People have their faith strengthened and deepened by miracles, and many people actually come to faith through miracles. My own [Eric Metaxas] conversion to faith is an example of this, as I relate later in this book (*Miracles*), and my faith has been dramatically strengthened by miracles that I have experienced personally, as well as by miracles that have happened to people I've known and whose judgement I've trusted."[52]

"Miracles are not a contradiction of nature. They are only in contradiction of what we know of nature."

– Saint Augustine

Miracles All Around Us

Those who are true to themselves must admit, if they are serious about it, that almost all things under the sun are, indeed, miracles.

---

51 Metaxas, *Miracles,* 53-55.

52 Metaxas, *Miracles,* 17.

The sun, the moon, the flowers growing in a field, the birds and fish in all their variety, a flash of lightning and an earthquake, wild animals and we humans, the miraculous birth of every human being, and our human bodies—that we are finding more about each year.

We are walking miracles; our human bodies are miracles.

BODY CELLS: *All of our body cells are regenerating themselves every day without your even knowing it. New set of taste buds every ten days, new nails every six to ten months, new bones every ten years, and even a new heart every twenty years.*

BODY ENERGY: *Your body is always producing work—and energy. And your extra energy is expelled by heat every second.*

BODY GROWTH: *Although you do not know it, your body grows a little every night while you sleep. But then again, your body shrinks back a little during the day, although you are not aware of it. Net change is close to zero.*

BRAIN: *Your brain is always working, even when you sleep. With the help of your brain, you are having up to forty-eight thoughts every minute.*

BREATH: *Your lungs hold about one and ½ gallons of air. And that means you must take about 17,000 breaths in the course of a day to keep your body functioning.*

DIGESTION: *In digestion you know that your stomach works hard, but you are not sure how hard. It takes up to eight hours for food to remain in the stomach and then up to two days overall to complete the digestion process.*

EYES: *Your eyes are important. They are one of the most complex organs in your body. Just to keep them healthy and moist, with involuntary reflex you blink up to 29,000 times every day, and you don't even notice it.*

HAIR: *Your hair on your head is always growing—that is, if you still have any. You are not aware of it, but it grows about ¼ inch per day.*

HEART: *You are not aware of it, but your heart is working hard every day—even when you are sleeping. In a typical day, it beats 100,000 times pumping 2,000 gallons of blood through your arteries every day.*

KIDNEY: *You have two kidneys (each the size of your fist) that contain tiny filters that filter and clean more than two pints of blood every minute. Also, another job is to expel about 2 ½ pints of urine every day.*

LIVER: *Your liver is like a factory plant inside your body. It manufactures cholesterol, vitamin D, and blood plasma; it stores away the nutrients the body needs for daily use; and it produces bile every day to help you break down your food.*

MOUTH: *The mouth has a big job to do, and it wouldn't be able to do that if it was not healthy 24/7. By producing about 3 pints of saliva every day, it is kept moist and not overrun by destructive bacteria.*

RED BLOOD CELLS: *Your red blood cells are the 'life' of your body delivering oxygen to keep it energized. A red blood cell makes 1,440 trips around your body every day.*

SKIN CELLS: *Did you know that your skin is the largest organ that you have with an average total surface of 18 square feet? You do not realize it, but to retain your overall health, you must shed one million old cells every day and replace them with new ones.*

STOMACH: *Your stomach accomplishes a major feat every time you eat a meal. It produces stomach acids to perform your food digestion. To keep your stomach acids from digesting your stomach wall (which would be a* *death sentence), your stomach lining produces an alkaline substance every few seconds to neutralize the stomach acid.*

As you do not know the path of the wind, or how the body is formed in a mother's womb, so you cannot understand the work of God, the Maker of all things

(ECCLESIASTES 11:5, NIV)

"I have said for years that speculations about the origin of life lead to no useful purpose as even the simplest living system is far too complex to be understood in terms of the extremely primitive chemistry scientists have used in their attempts to explain the unexplainable that happened 'billions' of years ago. God cannot be explained away by such naïve thoughts."

(Ernst Chain (world famous biochemist)[53]

What Are the Social Consequences of Belief in Evolution?

There are many!

The belief in evolution does matter! Walt Brown, in his book, *In the Beginning: Compelling Evidence for Creation and the Flood"*[54] enumerated a list of thirteen social consequences of belief in evolution. They are:

1. **Animal-like Behavior:** If humans descended from animals, <u>why shouldn't humans behave like animals?</u>
2. **Meaninglessness:** If evolution happened, <u>why believe that life has any purpose other than to reproduce and pass on your genes?</u>

---

[53] Ronald W. Clark, *The Life of Ernst Chain: Penicillin and Beyond* (London: Weidenfeld & Nicolson, 1985), 148.

[54] Brown, *In the Beginning*, 399–400. Used by permission.

3. **Good vs. Evil:** If nature is all there is, <u>why believe there is good and evil?</u>

4. **Survival of the Fittest:** If we evolved by "survival of the fittest," <u>then getting rid of the unfit is desirable.</u> To conquer and exploit weaker people, businesses, or countries is just the law of the jungle from which we evolved. Mercy killings, forced sterilization, and selective breeding of humans, while unpopular with some, would be beneficial, in the long run, and very logical—if we evolved.

5. **Communism:** Friedrich Engels, one of the founders of communism, wrote Karl Marx, another founder, and strongly recommended Charles Darwin's book *The Origin of Species.* In response, Marx wrote Engels that Darwin's book "*contains the basis in natural history for our view* (communism)."

6. **Personal Responsibility:** If everything came into existence by chance and natural processes, then <u>we have no responsibility to some supernatural being. Religions would be a crutch for the weak-minded and superstitious. Churches would be monuments to human ignorance.</u>

7. **Relativism:** There are <u>no absolutes, moral or otherwise</u> (except the fact that there are absolutely no absolutes). Your belief is just as good as mine; your truth is just as good as my truth.

8. **Social Darwinism:** If life evolved, <u>then the human mind evolved. So did products of the human mind and all social institutions: law, government, science, education, religion, language, economics, industry—civilization itself.</u>

9. **Secular Humanism:** If the "molecules-to-monkeys-to man" idea is correct, then man is the highest form of being. <u>Man should be the object of greatest concern, not some fictitious Creator that man actually created.</u>

10. **New Age Movement:** If people slowly evolved up from bacteria, then aren't we evolving toward God? Aren't we evolving a new consciousness? <u>Aren't we evolving into a glorious New Age?</u>

11. **Marriage:** If marriage is a cultural development, begun by ignorant tribes thousands of years ago, then why not change that custom, as we do other out-of-date customs? <u>Animals don't marry; why should people? After all, we're just animals. If people are a product of natural processes, then why not do what comes naturally? What's wrong with sexual activity outside of marriage as long as no one gets hurt?</u>

12. **Racism:** If humans evolved up from some apelike creature, then some people must have advanced higher on the evolutionary ladder than others. <u>Some classes of people should be inherently superior to others.</u>

13. **Abortion:** We dispose of unwanted animals such as dogs and cats. If humans are evolved animals, why not terminate an unwanted pregnancy? Isn't it the mother's right? Shouldn't she have a "choice" in such a personal matter? After all, a fetus has no name or personality. During its first three months, it's just a tiny glob of tissue—no more important than a little pig or rabbit. <u>Why shouldn't a fetus, having less value than an adult, be "terminated" if adults or society would benefit? This will help solve our population problem. We must guide our destiny.</u>

Also, in the book *A Dance with Deception, Charles Colson* states,

"The lesson of history is clear: when Christian belief is strong, the crime rate falls; when Christian belief weakens, the crime rate climbs. Widespread religious belief creates a shared social ethic that acts as a restraint on the dark side of human nature."[55]

---

[55] Charles Colson W., *A Dance with Deception* (Nashville: W Publishing Group, 2004), 190.

There is a God

Antony Flew, one of the world's most notorious atheists, changed his mind. He started out believing there is no God. Now he knows there is a God. He quoted his friend Ralph McInerny,

> "The Thomist philosopher Ralph McInerny reasoned that it is natural for human beings to believe in God because of the order, arrangement, and law-like character of natural events. So much so, he said, that the idea of God is almost innate, which seems like a prima facie argument against atheism. So, while Plantings argued that theists did not bear the burden of the proof, McInerny went still further, holding that **the burden of proof must fall on atheists!**"[56]

---

[56] Antony Flew, *There Is a God: How the World's Most Notorious Atheist Changed His Mind* (San Francisco: Harper One, 2007), 55-56.

THE SCIENTIFIC DISCUSSION
AND "THE ARGUMENT"

This section will be presented based primarily on Dr. Duane Gish's seven areas of comparison between the "**Creation Model**" and the "**Evolution Model.**" [57]

2.1 Formation of Earth's Geographical Features

2.2 Life on Earth – Thousands of Years or Billions of Years?

2.3 Use of Radiometric and Other Dating to Get Accurate Results of Age

2.4 Emergence of Plants and Animals: What the Fossil Record Shows

2.5 Mutations: Are they Good or Bad?

2.6 Man and Apes: Their Separate Ancestry

2.7 Emergence of the Universe and the Solar System

---

[57] Gish, "Summary of Scientific Evidence for Creation (Part I & II)."

2.1 Formation of Earth's Geological Features

We start with Dr. Duane Gish's take on the formation of the earth's geological features (VI).

Creation Model: <u>The earth's geologic features appear to have been fashioned largely by rapid, catastrophic processes that affected the earth on a global and regional scale (catastrophism).</u>

Evolution Model: The earth's geologic features were fashioned largely by slow, gradual processes, with infrequent catastrophic events restricted to a local scale (uniformitarianism).

The Creation View: Catastrophic events have characterized the earth's history. Huge floods, massive asteroid collisions, large volcanic eruptions, devastating landslides, and intense earthquakes have left their marks on the earth. Uniform processes such as normal river sedimentation, small volcanoes, slow erosion, and small earthquakes appear insufficient to explain large portions of the geologic record. http://www.icr.org/article/summary-scientific-evidence-for-creation/ (VI)

Mount St. Helens – Evidence for Genesis

The following is an excerpted commentary by Ken Ham of Answers in Genesis (AiG) which was submitted in May 2000 to a few newspapers in the United States to commemorate the twentieth anniversary of the eruption of Mount St. Helens in America's Pacific Northwest:

> *"As I stood staring at the incredible geologic features that resulted from the May 18, 1980, eruption of Mount St. Helens in Washington State, I was reminded afresh of how small and vulnerable we are as humans, but how awesome must be the power of God who created earth and its mountains.*

. . . .

What struck me even more was that the study of the eruption and its after-effects has challenged the very foundations of evolution theory.

. . . .

The events associated with the volcano's explosion accomplished in seconds, hours, or just a few days, geologic work that normally would be interpreted as having taken hundreds or even millions of years. One particular canyon was formed, which has since been named the "Little Grand Canyon." About 100 feet deep and somewhat wider, it is about 1/40th the scale of the mighty Grand Canyon. This canyon was formed in one day from a mudflow. A newly formed river then flowed through the Canyon formed by the mudflow.

. . . .

People around the world are indoctrinated by evolutionists who believe that layers like those we see at the Grand Canyon took millions of years to be laid down. That belief of "billions of years" is foundational to evolutionary thinking. What happened at Mount St. Helens is a powerful challenge to this belief.

The evidence here shows that one can logically accept that the Flood of Noah's day—and its after-effects—could have accomplished extraordinary geological work, carving out canyons and the laying down of sediments in massive quantities all across the globe—just as we see today!" [58]

---

[58] Ken Ham, "Mount St. Helens—Evidence for Genesis!" Answers in Genesis, May 17, 2000. Used by permission. https://answersingenesis.org/geology/mount-st-helens/mount-st-helens-evidence-for-genesis/.

The Yellowstone Petrified Forests – Evidence of Catastrophe

Dr. Jonathan Sarfati, of Creation Ministries International (CMI), wrote about Yellowstone National Park some time back:

> *"Yellowstone National Park, the oldest national park in the United States, spans parts of three states: Wyoming, Montana, and Idaho. It is famous for its geothermal activity, including 10,000 hot springs and 200 geysers, including Old Faithful. There are also mountains, including one of black obsidian (volcanic glass), cooled and hardened basalt lava flows, deep valleys and canyons, rivers, lakes, forests, petrified wood (wood turned into rock), and wildlife.*

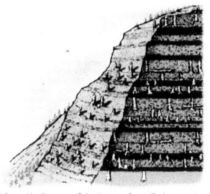

Diagram used with permission from *The Young Earth* by John D. Morris.

Schematic diagram of the layers of petrified trees at Yellowstone.

> *In some places in Yellowstone Park, erosion of a hillside reveals layers of upright petrified trees. At Specimen Ridge, there are said to be 27 layers, while Specimen Creek contains about 50. This means that the Specimen Creek formation is especially huge—its total vertical height is 1,000 meters (3,400 feet). This raises the question: how did the petrified tree layers form?"* [59]

---

[59]   Jonathan Sarfati, "The Yellowstone petrified forests: Evidence of catastrophe," Creation Ministries International, March 21, 1999, accessed November 8, 2018, https://creation.com/the-yellowstone-petrified-forests. Used by permission of Creation Ministries International. Offices in 6 countries including Atlanta, Georgia. All rights reserved.

Note: The experience at Mount St. Helens gives a clue.[60] Read about it and find out.

Catastrophism Gaining Acceptance Now

Harold Coffin, author of *Origin by Design,* noted that:

> "If catastrophism (along with uniformitarianism) had exerted its influence in geological research during the past 100 years, the state of the science now would be further along. But geology is giving the role of catastrophe (on a local scale especially) more attention now. **Studies of the Grand Canyon and examination of pictures taken by John Wesley Powell more than 100 years ago show that almost nothing happened to the canyon during that time except where a flash flood recently reshaped a section of a tributary canyon in a few hours.**"[61]

2.2 Life on Earth—Thousands of Years or Billions of Years?

Let's look at Dr. Duane Gish's take on how long it took for life to emerge on our Earth (II).[62]

<u>Creation Model:</u> Life was suddenly created.

Evolution Model: Life emerged from nonlife by naturalistic processes.

---

[60]   Ham, "Mount St. Helens."

[61]   Harold G. Coffin and Robert H. Brown, *Origin by Design* (Hargerstown, MD: Review & Herald Publishing, 2005), 109.

[62]   Gish, "Summary of Scientific Evidence for Creation (Part I & II)."

The Creation View: Life appears abruptly and in complex forms in the fossil record, and gaps appear systematically in the fossil record between various living kinds. The laboratory experiments related to theories on the origin of life have not even remotely approached the synthesis of life from nonlife, and the extremely limited results have depended on laboratory conditions that are artificially imposed and extremely improbable. The extreme improbability of these conditions and the relatively insignificant results apparently show that life did not emerge by the process that evolutionists postulate.

Two Timelines of the History of our World

The Evolutionary Timeline vs. the Biblical Timeline

It is time, such as it were, to try to compare the timelines of the two views. And they couldn't be further apart—in time. The evolutionary timeframe, from an average of a number of sources, is about 4.5 billions of years for the existence of our world. The Biblical timeframe, from an average of a number of sources, is about six thousand years for the existence of the world.

In simple terms, the difference is caused because **evolutionists believe it took billions of years for life to *evolve* (based on *chance*)** from the simplest life ... to advanced life ... to animals ... and then to Man. **The Creation model contends that the God of all life (based on *miracles*) created Earth—and all life—in six 24-hour days—about six thousand years ago.**

See the comparative figures, "Two Timelines of History."

(The first is a construct of the author, Jay Schabacker)

TWO TIME LINES OF HISTORY

BIBLICAL TIMELINE
(Dates are average of a number of sources)

Thousands of Years Ago (BC)

Creation of the World	4,088
Birth of Noah	3,018
The worldwide flood	2,427
The Tower of Babel	2,267
The Epic of Gilgamesh	2,150
Call of Abraham	1,926
The Pyramid of Giza	1,650
Hebrews Exodus from Egypt	1,481
Foundation of the Temple Laid	990
Birth of Christ	4

MILLIONS OF YEARS AGO (BC)

Earth Formed Hadean Era	4,543 Million Years Ago (4.5 Billion Years Ago) Earliest Earth, Water
Precamberian Period Archean Era	3,513 Million Years Ago (3.5 Million Years Ago) Single Celled Life, Microbes, Bacteria, Green Algae
Cambrian Period Paleozoic Era	547 Million Years Ago Invertebrates, Sponges, Brachiopods, Trilobites, Jellyfish, Worms
Devonian Period Paleozoic Era	410 Million Years Ago Amphibians, First Boney Fish, Mollusks
Permian Period Paleozoic Era	263 Million Years Ago Ferns, Insects, Reptiles, Large Amphibians, Seed Plants
Triassic Period Mesozoic Era	249 Million Years Ago Boney Fish Diversify, Dinosaurs, Primitive Mammals
Jurassic Period Mesozoic Era	193 Million Years Ago First Mammals and Birds, Flying Reptiles, First Flowering Plants
Cretaceous Period Mesozoic Era	144 Million Years Ago Modern Seed Bearing Plants, Birds Well Developed Extinction of Dinosaurs
Paleocene Period Cenozoic Era	65 Million Years Ago Grazing Mammals, Rise of Primates, Mammal Carnivores
Miocene Period Cenozoic Era	23 Million Years Ago Whales, Apes, Spread of Grasslands, and Grazing Mammals
Pliocene Period Cenozoic Era	5 Million Years Ago Large Carnivores, Humanlike Primates
Pleistocene Epoch Cenozoic Era	2 Million Years Ago First Hominids Appear, Homo Sapiens, Era of Ice Ages
Quaternary Period Holocene Epoch	11 Thousand Years Ago Modern Human Worldwide Distribution, Humans Spread Across America, All Islands

EVOLUTIONARY TIMELINE
(Dates are average of a number of sources)

The Two Timelines of History

Standard Timeline (years)

Big Bang | Onset of Huronian Ice Age | Begin First Dynasty | Imhotep 2700 | Collapse of Egypt 2200/ 1800 | Thutmose III 1450

13.7 b   2.4 b   10000 3000   600   0   Now

End Ice Age

« BC/BCE | AD/CE »

Biblical Timeline (years)

Creation | Noah's Flood | Abraham In Egypt | 800 | Birth of Christ

5500   3300   2500 1900   0   Now

Solomon 950
Exodus 1450
Joseph 1700
Abraham in Egypt

One billion = one thousand million
BC = Before Christ   AD = Anno Domini
BCE = Before Common Era
CE = Common Era
Creation and Noah's Flood on Septuagint timeline   A. Habermehl 2015

Dr. Henry M. Morris, in his book, *Science and the Bible*, states:

"All such processes that go back beyond the beginning of recorded history (say, five thousand years or so) necessarily involve assumptions that cannot be tested. But the assumptions that lead to a young earth are far more reasonable and conservative than the assumptions on which uranium dating and other such radiometric methods are based. And the numbers of processes that yield a young age exceed by far the very few processes favored by evolutionists because they yield an old age."[63]

---

[63]   Morris, *Science and the Bible*, 90.

Some Fossil Evidence

Again, Dr. Henry M. Morris in *Science and the Bible* states,

> *"One of the most obvious indications of catastrophism is in the vast fossil graveyard in the sedimentary rock column, averaging a mile deep all around the globe. The very existence of fossils indicates rapid burial of the organisms, followed by rapid compaction of the sediments encasing them, else they would not have been preserved at all.* **Yet fossils are found everywhere by the billions.***"*[64]

"Many fish were buried alive (in the flood) and fossilized quickly, such as the fish "caught in the act" of eating its last meal."[65]

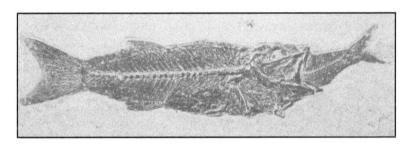

Photo by Dr. Andrew Snelling. Used by permission.

Some Other Problems with the Evolutionary Timeline

Out-of-Sequence Fossils 1: Frequently, fossils are not vertically sequenced in the assumed evolutionary order.

Out-of-Sequence Fossils 2: In Uzbekistan, eighty-six consecutive hoof-prints of horses were found in rocks dating back to the dinosaurs. A

---

[64] Morris, *Science and the Bible*, 77.

[65] Dr. Andrew A. Snelling, "The World's a Graveyard: Flood Evidence Number Two," Answers in Genesis, February 12, 2008, https://answersingenesis.org/fossils/fossil-record/the-worlds-a-graveyard/. Used by permission.

leading authority on the Grand Canyon published photographs of horse-like hoofprints visible in rocks that, according to the theory of evolution, predate hoofed animals by more than 100 million years.

Out-of-Sequence Fossils 3: Sometimes land animals, flying animals, and marine animals are fossilized side-by-side in the same rock. Dinosaur, whale, elephant, horse, and other fossils, plus crude human tools, have reportedly been found in phosphate beds in South Carolina. Coal beds contain round, black lumps called *coal balls*, some of which contain flowering plants that allegedly evolved 100 million years after the coal bed was formed.

Out-of-Sequence Fossils 4: Amber, found in Illinois coal beds, contain chemical signatures showing that the amber came from flowering plants, but flowering plants supposedly evolved 170 million years after the coal formed. In the Grand Canyon, in Venezuela, in Kashmir, and in Guyana, spores of ferns and pollen from flowering plants are found in Cambrian rocks—rocks supposedly deposited before flowering plants evolved. Pollen has also been found in Precambrian rocks deposited before life allegedly evolved.

Out-of-Sequence Fossils 5: Petrified trees in Arizona's Petrified Forest National Park contain fossilized nests of bee and cocoons of wasps. The petrified forests are reputedly 220 million years old, while bees (and flowering plants, which bees require) supposedly evolved almost 100 million years later. Pollinating insects and fossil flies, with long, well-developed tubes for sucking nectar from flowers, are dated 25 million years before flowers are assumed to have evolved. **Most evolutionists and textbooks systematically ignore discoveries which conflict with the evolutionary time scale.**[66]

---

[66]   Brown, *In the Beginning*, 12.

"All paleontologists know that the fossil record contains precious little in the way of intermediate forms; transitions between major groups are characteristically abrupt."

(Gould, Stephen J. [Professor of Geology and Paleontology, Harvard University])[67]

The fossilized tree shown in the picture below was located in Nova Scotia, photographed by Michael C. Rygel:

Photo: Michael C. Rygel via Wikimedia Commons

2.3 Use of Radiometric and Other Dating to Get Accurate Results of Age

Let's look at Dr. Duane Gish's take on the use of radiometric age dating and other methods and the results assumed (VII).[68]

Creation Model: The inception of the earth and of living kinds may have been relatively recent.

---

[67] Stephen Jay Gould, *The Panda's Thumb* (New York: W. W. Norton & Company, 1980), 189.

[68] Gish, "Summary of Scientific Evidence for Creation (Part I & II)," VII.

Evolution Model: The inception of the earth and then of life must have occurred several billion years ago.

The Creation View: Numerous radiometric estimates have been hundreds of millions of years in excess of the true age. Thus ages estimated by the radiometric dating methods may very well be grossly in error. Extrapolating the observed rate of apparently exponential decay of the earth's magnetic field, the age of the earth or life seemingly could not exceed 20,000 years. Thus the inception of the earth and the inception of life may have been relatively recent when all evidence is considered.

Per the C-14/C-12 radiometric dating method, graphed below[69], the evolutionists, using the Normal Assumption **get millions or billions of years of age**; the creationist scientists using changes based on The Flood **get a much more recent date.**

---

[69] Brown, *In the Beginning,* Figure 178, 343. Used by permission.

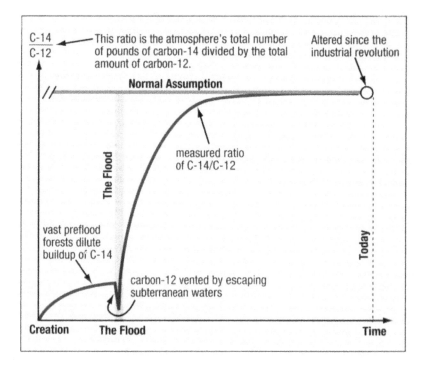

What about the C14 Carbon dating of Objects in the Geologic Column?

C14 is unstable and slowly decays, changing back into nitrogen and releasing energy. As soon as a plant or animal dies, the C14 atoms which decay are no longer replaced, so the amount of C14 from once living things decreases as time goes on. Anything over about 50,000 years old should theoretically have no detectable C14 left. That is why radiocarbon dating cannot give millions of years. **In fact, if a sample contains C14, it is good evidence that it is *not* millions of years old.**[70]

In the typical fossil record 'Geological Column' as depicted by evolutionary scientists, **the remains dug up all contain amounts of C14 showing they are *not* millions of years old.**

---

[70] David Catchpoole et al., *The Creation Answers Book* (Powder Springs, GA: Creation Book Publishers, 2017), 66-67.

"In fact, evolution became in a sense a scientific religion; almost all scientists have accepted it and many are prepared to 'bend' their observations to fit in with it."

(H.S. Lipson, FRS (Professor of Physics,
University of Manchester, UK)[71]

2.4 Emergence of Plants and Animals: What the Fossil Record Shows

Again, let's look at Dr. Duane Gish's take on the emergence of all life on the earth: plants, animals, humans—and how long it took (III).

Creation Model: All present living kinds of animals and plants have remained fixed since creation, other than extinctions, and genetic variations in originally created kinds have only occurred within narrow limits.

Evolution Model: All present kinds emerged from simpler earlier kinds, so that single-celled organisms evolved into invertebrates, then vertebrates, then amphibians, then reptiles, then mammals, then primates, including man.

The Creation View: Systematic gaps occur between kinds in the fossil record. None of the intermediate fossils that would be expected on the basis of the evolution model have been found between single celled organisms and invertebrates, between invertebrates and vertebrates, between fish and amphibians, between amphibians and reptiles, between reptiles and birds or mammals, or between "lower" mammals and primates. http://www.icr.org/article/summary-scientific-evidence-for-creation/ (III)

---

[71] H.S. Lipson, "A physicist looks at evolution," *Physics Bulletin* 31 (1980): 138.

Romer's Gap

Evolutionists have long noted "Romer's Gap," an absence of terrestrial fossils in 15 million years' worth of rock in the geological column above the Devonian mass extinction of aquatic animals. A trove of terrestrial fossils in Scotland discovered by Stanley Wood and Jennifer Clark "is forcing archeologists the world over to do some rewriting of their history books."

Evolutionary paleontologists have pondered whether there really was a multimillion-year gap (from 360 million years ago to 345 million) after the death of so many aquatic creatures before evolution could move forward. Perhaps they just hadn't found enough fossils yet. The gap used to be 30 million years when vertebrate paleontologist Alfred Romer first noticed the hole in the fossil record. Since then, fossil finds have supposedly partially filled in. With Clark and Wood's discoveries, the gap disappears.

Romer's gap, if it contained any fossils, should in the evolutionary view reveal transitions between aquatic and terrestrial animals. As Clark explains, "The break has been frustrating, because you wouldn't expect evolution to jump from simple aquatic creatures to complex, terrestrial animals without something in between."[72]

> *The picture that emerges from the fossil record is completely compatible with creation. The record reveals that living things appeared suddenly and lived for long periods of time without undergoing any change at all.*

The Coelacanth Phenomenon

It is significant that some fossilized animals and plants once thought to be extinct have in fact been found still alive, thus demonstrating the total

---

[72]   Dr. Elizabeth Mitchell, "Fossil Gap Closes More Missing Links," Answers in Genesis, March 10, 2012, https://answersingenesis.org/fossils/transitional-fossils/fossil-gap-closes-more-missing-links/. Used by permission.

unreliability of the evolutionary time scale. The last fossilized coelacanth (a fish) is supposedly 65 million years old, but coelacanths are still here, so where did they "hide" for 65 million years?

Reconstruction of West Indian Ocean Coelacanth
Photo: "Latimeria chalumnae replica"
by Citron / CC-BY-SA-3.0 via Wikimedia Commons

The Wollemi pine's last fossil is supposedly 150 million years old, but identical living trees were found in 1994. The recent burial and fossilization of these animals and plants, and the extinction of many other animals and plants, during the single biblical flood thus makes better sense of all the fossil and geological evidence.[73]

In a lengthy article by Alex Williams, "What life is,"[74] he gives a couple of short summaries:

- *The materialistic view of life as a natural phenomenon has been deeply contradicted by research into its molecular mechanics.*
- *It is indefensible. Only Genesis-style fiat creation can explain it.*

---

[73] Ken Ham, *The New Answers Book 2* (Green Forest, AR: Master Books, 2008), 345.

[74] Alex Williams, "What Life Is," Creation Ministries International, December 2015, https://creation.com/what-life-is.

The Record of Rock Strata

Numerous rock strata have given scientists geological and fossil clues. Here are just a few well-known locations:

1. Ashley Phosphate Beds of South Carolina
2. Beartooth Butte Uplift, Wyoming
3. Cadillac Mountain, Acadia National Park
4. Columbia River Basalt Flows
5. Colorado River Canyon
6. European Alps – Mountain Building
7. Fossil Trilobites (pill buglike animals) from the Burgess Shale
8. Grand Canyon Geology Formation Column
9. Green River Formation of Wyoming
10. Heart Mountain Thrust
11. Himalayan Mountains
12. Long Island Sand and Sediments
13. Mount St. Helens
14. Mowry Shale Wyoming – fish scales
15. Po River Delta in Italy
16. Saskatchewan Badlands Erosion
17. Yellowstone Park Petrified Forests

"It is easy enough to make up stories of how one form gave rise to another, and to find reasons why the stages should be favored by natural selection. But such stories are not a part of science, for there is no way of putting them to the test."[75]
(Personal letter written 10 April 1979 from Dr. Colin Patterson, Senior Palaeontologist at the British Museum of Natural History in London, to Luther D. Sunderland; as quoted in Darwin's Enigma *by Luther D. Sunderland)*

---

[75] Luther D. Sunderland, *Darwin's Enigma* (Green Forest, AR: Master Books, 1981), 198.

2.5   Mutations: Are They Good or Bad?

Let's look at Dr. Duane Gish's take on mutations and natural selection, i.e., Evolution (IV).[76]

Creation Model: Mutation and natural selection are insufficient to have brought about any emergence of present living kinds from a simple primordial organism.

Evolution Model: Mutation and natural selection have brought about the emergence of present complex kinds from a simple primordial organism.

The Creation View: The mathematical probability that random mutation and natural selection ultimately produced complex living kinds from a similar kind is infinitesimally small even after many billions of years. Thus natural selection seemingly does not provide a testable explanation of how mutations would produce more fit organisms.

> "Why Mutations Cannot Produce Cross-Species Change"
> A mutation is damage to a single DNA unit (a gene)…. Mutations rank equally with fossils and natural selection as the three most important aspects of life evolution…. So that brings us to mutations. The study of mutations is crucial! It is all that the evolutionists have left! If mutations cannot produce evolution, then nothing can.

. . . .

The Last Hope—It is well known among many knowledgeable scientists that if evolution could possibly occur, mutations would have to accomplish it. There simply is no other mechanism that can make changes within the

---

[76]   Gish, "Summary of Scientific Evidence for Creation (Part I & II)," IV.

DNA. Natural selection has consistently failed, so mutations are the last hope of a majority of the evolutionists today.... Neo-Darwinists speculate that mutations accomplished all cross-species changes, and then natural selection afterward refined them. This, of course, assumes that mutation and natural selection are positive and purposive.

. . . .

In reality, mutations have four special qualities that are ruinous to the hopes of evolutionists:

1. **Rare Effects**—Mutations are very rare. This point is not a guess but a scientific fact, observed by experts in the field. Their very rarity dooms the possibility of mutational evolution to oblivion.
2. **Random Effects**—Mutations are always random, and never purposive or directed. This has repeatedly been observed in actual experimentation with mutations.
3. **Not Helpful**—Evolution requires improvement. Mutations do not help or improve; they only weaken and injure.
4. **Harmful Effects**—Nearly all mutations are harmful. In most instances, mutations weaken or damage the organism in some way so that it (or its offspring if it is able to have any) will not long survive.[77]

"The ability to duplicate accurately would seem to be impossible, short of a complicated system like DNA. Evolutionists working earnestly to explain the origins of life would sometimes make vague references to proteins serving as TEMPLATES or patterns on which copies like themselves

---

[77] Pathlights, "Chapter 10a: Mutations — Why Mutations cannot Produce Cross-species Change," accessed November 8, 2018, http://pathlights.com/ce_encyclopedia/sci-ev/sci_vs_ev_10.htm.

could form. No way has been found to make such outcomes occur.[78]

Genetic Entropy

Newsflash—Mutations/selections cannot even create a single gene.

Dr. John Sanford, a geneticist and past professor at Cornell University, wrote an acclaimed book, "Genetic Entropy & the Mystery of the Genome." (On the back of the book jacket you will find recommendations from Dr. Michael Behe, Dr. John Baumgardner, Dr. Henry Morris, and Professor Phillip Johnson).

Dr. Sanford takes issue with the evolutionary scientists' 'Primary Axiom'—the idea that man is merely the product of random mutations plus natural selection. Through analysis, Dr. Sanford destroys this theory. In answer to the question, 'Are mutations good?' his answer is definitely 'No'! He states in the book, page 27, "In conclusion, mutations appear to be overwhelmingly deleterious, and even when one may be classified as beneficial in some specific sense, it is still usually part of an over-all breakdown and erosion of information."

Those who like figures and graphs might want to review his "Genetic Entropy" figures which follow.[79]

---

[78] James F. Coppedge, *Evolution: Possible or Impossible?* (Grand Rapids: Zondervan, 1973), 92.

[79] Dr. J. C. Sanford, *Genetic Entropy and the Mystery of the Genome Classroom Edition*, 3rd edition (Massachusetts: Feed My Sheep Foundation, Inc., 2008), Figures 3a-3d, 27, 29-32. Used by permission.

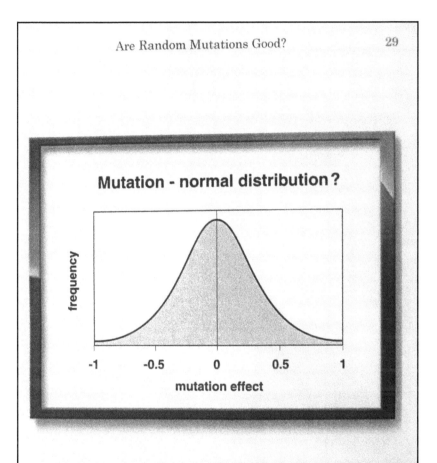

Figure 3a.

The naive view of mutations would be a bell-shaped distribution, with half of all mutations showing deleterious affects on fitness (left of center), and half showing positive effects on fitness (right of center). With such a distribution it would be easy to imagine selection removing bad mutations and fixing good mutations, inevitably resulting in evolutionary progress. However, we know this is a false picture.

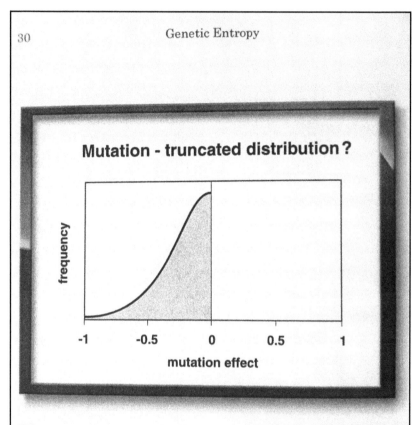

Figure 3b.

Population geneticists know that essentially all mutations are deleterious, and that mutations having positive effects on fitness are so rare as to be excluded from such distribution diagrams. This creates major problems for evolutionary theory. But this picture is still too optimistic.

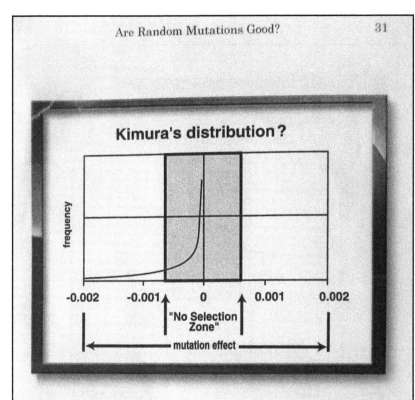

Figure 3c.

Population geneticists know that mutations are strongly skewed toward neutral. Just like in an instruction manual, a few misspellings will be lethal but most will be *nearly harmless*. The nearly-neutral mutations create the biggest problems for evolutionary theory. This diagram is adapted from a figure by Kimura (1979). Kimura is famous for showing that most mutations are nearly neutral, and therefore are not subject to selection. Kimura's "no-selection zone" is shown by the box.

The general shape of this curve is important, but the precise mathematical nature of this curve is not. While Ohta feels the mutation distribution is exponential, Kimura feels it is a 'gamma' distribution (Kimura, 1979). However, regardless of which specific mathematical formulation best describes the natural distribution of mutation effects, they all approximate the picture shown above.

For your possible interest, geneticists agree that the frequency of highly deleterious mutations is almost zero (not shown, off the chart), while "minor" mutations are intermediate in frequency (i.e., the left portion of chart, and off chart). Minor mutations are believed to outnumber major mutations by about 10-50 fold (Crow, 1997), but near-neutrals vastly outnumber them both.

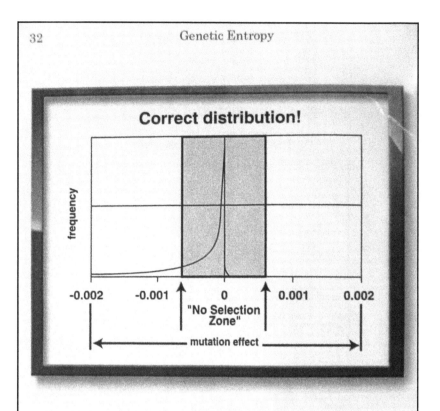

Figure 3d.

Kimura's Figure (3c) is still not complete. To complete the figure we really must show where the beneficial mutations would occur, as they are critical to evolutionary theory. Their distribution would be a reverse image of Kimura's curve, but reduced in range and scale, by a factor of somewhere between ten thousand to one million. Because of the scale of this diagram, I cannot draw this part of the mutation distribution small enough, so a relatively large triangle is shown instead. Even with beneficial mutations greatly exaggerated, it becomes obvious that essentially all beneficial mutations will fall within Kimura's "no-selection zone". This completed picture, which is correct, makes progressive evolution on the genomic level virtually impossible.

Media Silent on Genetic Study Defying Evolution

Secular research found 90 percent of animal species appeared at same time as humans

When a scientific study was published showing that 90 percent of animals appeared on the Earth at the same time as humans, you could almost hear the proverbial pin drop in the popular press, academia, and the evolutionary scientific community.

Since then, not one major news agency has reported the shocking findings. There has not been any significant attempt at refutation of the research by the evolutionary scientific community. There are no reports of an uproar in the science academy.

Researcher and coauthor Dr. David Thaler: "The conclusion is very surprising, and I fought against it as hard as I could,"[80]

Recent mitochondrial DNA barcoding results bode well for the recent origin of species,
by Dr. Nathaniel T. Jeanson on July 27, 2018

A recent review paper proposed a controversial claim—that the vast majority of animal species arose contemporary with modern humans. Not surprisingly, this claim was met with backlash from the evolutionary community. On what basis did the authors make this wide-reaching claim? Is their assertion true? Furthermore, what ramifications do their data have for the creationist explanation of the origin of species from the originally created min or "kinds"?

The main focus of Dr. Stoeckle and Dr. Thaler's paper is genetics. Specifically, they focus on a subset of DNA in humans and animal cells, termed mitochondrial DNA (mtDNA). Their analysis of the mtDNA is

---

[80] https://www.wnd.com/2018/07/media-silent-on-genetic-study-defying-evolution

clear, straightforward, and carefully justified—so much so that I will summarize their arguments by liberally quoting from their paper.

Barcoding and the Origin of Species: Stoeckle and Thaler recognize the sweeping potential in these patterns: "The agreement of barcodes and domain experts implies that explaining the origin of the pattern of DNA barcodes would be in large part explaining the origin of species. Understanding the mechanism by which the near-universal pattern of DNA barcodes comes about would be tantamount to understanding the mechanism of speciation."

In their evolutionary model, Stoeckle and Thaler invoke two hypotheses to account for the barcode cluster of patterns: "Either 1) COI barcode clusters represent species-specific adaptations, OR 2) extant populations have recently passed through diversity-reducing regimes whose consequences for sequence diversity are indistinguishable from clonal bottlenecks."

Their conclusion? "Modern human mitochondria and Y chromosome (another subset of DNA, but inherited paternally) originated from conditions that imposed a single sequence of these genetic elements between 100,000 and 200,000 years ago." In other words, to account for human CO barcode patterns, they favor the second hypothesis—some sort of population dynamic (contraction) that reduced the genetic diversity of the population.

Stoeckle and Thaler then extrapolate their conclusions to controversial heights. To justify their extrapolation, they caution that "one should not as a first impulse seek a complex and multifaceted explanation for one of the clearest, most data rich and general facts in all evolution." Then they draw a parallel: "The simple hypothesis is that the same explanation offered for the sequence variation found among modern humans applies equally to the modern populations of essentially all other animal species; namely, that the extant population, no matter what its current size or similarity to fossils of any age, has expanded from mitochondrial uniformity within the past 200,000 years." In other words, based on mtDNA barcodes, Stoeckle and Thaler claim that the vast majority of species have originated contemporaneously with modern humans.[81]

Dr. Michael Guillen of Fox News gives an example of how mutation errors accumulate over time in reproduction, just like the errors in photocopying.

> *"Mark Stoeckle at Rockefeller University and David Thaler at the University of Basel reached the striking conclusion after analyzing the DNA 'bar codes' of five million animals from 100,00 different species. The bar codes are snippets of DNA that reside outside the nuclei of living cells—so-called mitochondrial DNA, which mothers pass down from generation to generation.* **With each reproduction, errors creep into the bar code, as they do when you repeatedly photocopy a document.** *By measuring the accumulated errors – the blurriness or 'diversity' among the bar codes—scientists are able to infer the passage of time."*[82]

Sweeping DNA Study Supports Creationism

What Stoeckle and Thaler found upends evolution theory and appears to support creationism in several ways. Stoeckle and Thaler reported that:

1. Species with large, far-flung populations—from ants, to rats, to humans—do not become more genetically diverse over time.
2. Nine out of 10 species on Earth today, including humans, came into being 100,000 to 200,000 years ago.

---

[81] https://answersingenesis.org/genetics/animal-genetics/hundreds-thousands-species-few-thousand-years/

[82] https://www.foxnews.com/opinion/did-a-mysterious-extinction-event-precede-adam-and-eve

3. In analyzing the bar codes across 100,000 species, they found a telltale sign showing that almost all the animals emerged about the same time as humans.

4. Species have very clear genetic boundaries, and there's nothing much in between.[83]

Genetic Research Keeps Confirming a Recent Creation

A massive new genetic study by secular scientists analyzed the DNA of over 100,000 animal species using about five million DNA sequences. When the researchers extrapolated this data into time frames of origins, they discovered about 90 percent of all animal life was roughly the same, very recent in age—a complete contradiction of evolutionary expectations. Mark Stoeckle, the other study author, remarked, "It is more likely that—at all times in evolution—the animals alive at that point arose relatively recently." *According to evolution, animals have progressively arisen over a half-billion years—not all at once in recent time.*[84]

---

[83]   https://drrichswier.com/2018/06/05/sweeping-dna-study-supports-creationism/

[84]   https://www.icr.org/article/genetics-research-keeps-confirming-recent-creation

2.6 Man and Apes: Their Separate Ancestry

Let's take a look at Dr. Duane Gish's take on man and apes and supposed linkages (V).[85]

Creation Model: Man and apes have a separate ancestry.

Evolution Model: Man and apes emerged from a common ancestor.

The Creation View: Although highly imaginative "transitional forms" between man and apelike creatures have been constructed by evolutionists based on very fragmentary evidence, the fossil record actually documents the separate origin of primates in general, monkeys, apes, and men.

Some Evolutionist Fakes and Frauds

In an attempt to further their careers and justify the claims that evolution is a legitimate theory, many scientists have fraudulently deceived the world. Here are just a few:

Piltdown man: Found in a gravel pit in Sussex England in 1912, this fossil was considered by some sources to be the second most important fossil proving the evolution of man—until it was found to be a complete forgery forty-one years later. The skull was found to be of modern age. The fragments had been chemically stained to give the appearance of age, and the teeth had been filed down!

Nebraska man: A single tooth discovered in Nebraska in 1922 grew an entire evolutionary link between man and monkey, until another identical tooth was found which was protruding from the jawbone of a wild pig.

---

[85] Gish, "Summary of Scientific Evidence for Creation (Part I & II)," V.

Java man: Initially discovered by Dutchman Eugene Dubois in 1891, all that was found of this claimed originator of humans was a skullcap, three teeth, and a femur. The femur was found 50 feet away from the original skullcap a full year later. Dubois downplayed the Wadjak skulls—two undoubtedly human skulls found very close to his "missing link."[86]

Orce man: Found in the southern Spanish town of Orce in 1982 and hailed as the oldest fossilized human remains ever found in Europe. One year later officials admitted the skull fragment was not human but probably came from a four-month-old donkey. Scientists had said the skull belonged to a seventeen-year-old man who lived 900,000 to 1.6 million years ago, and even had very detailed drawings done to represent what he would have looked like.[87]

Neanderthal: Still synonymous with brutishness, the first Neanderthal remains were found in France in 1908. Considered to be ignorant, ape-like, stooped, and knuckle-dragging, much of the evidence now suggests that Neanderthal was just as human as us, and his stooped appearance was because of arthritis and rickets. Neanderthals are now recognized as skillful hunters, believers in an afterlife, and even skilled surgeons, as seen in one skeleton whose withered right arm had been amputated above the elbow.[88]

Haekel's faked embryonic drawings: The theory of embryonic recapitulation asserts that the human fetus goes through various stages of its evolutionary history as it develops. Ernst Haeckel proposed this theory in the late 1860s, promoting Darwin's theory of evolution in Germany. He made detailed drawings of the embryonic development of eight different embryos in three stages of development to bolster his claim. His work was

---

[86] Hank Hanegraaff, *The Face That Demonstrates The Farce of Evolution* (Nashville: Word Publishing, 1998), 50–52.

[87] "Skull fragment may not be human," *Knoxville News-Sentinel*, 1983.

[88] "Upgrading Neanderthal Man," *Time Magazine*, May 17, 1971.

hailed as a great development in the understanding of human evolution. A few years later his drawings were shown to have been fabricated and the dates manufactured. He blamed the artist for the discrepancies, without admitting that he was the artist.[89]

Brontosaurus: One of the best known dinosaurs in books and museums for the past hundred years, brontosaurus, never really existed. The dinosaur's skeleton was found with a head missing. To complete it, a skull found three or four miles away was added. No one knew this for years. The body actually belonged to a species of Diplodocus and the head was from an Apatosaurus.[90]

Archaeoraptor Liaoningenis, Fake Dinosaur-bird ancestor: The most recent and perhaps the most infamous evolution frauds was committed in China and published in 1999 in the journal *National Geographic* 196:98–107, November 1999. Dinosaur bones were put together with the bone of a newer species of bird and they tried to pass it off as a very important new evolutionary intermediate.[91]

---

[89] Russell Grigg, "Fraud Rediscovered," *Journal of Creation* 20, no. 2, (April 1986): 49-51.

[90] Paul S. Taylor, *The Great Dinosaur Mystery and the Bible* (Chariot Victor Publishing, 1989), 12-13.

[91] Christopher P. Sloan, "Feathers For T-Rex?" *National Geographic Magazine*, November 1999.

Fake News: It Still Happens!

Fox News Reported (March 2018): "150M year-old dinosaur could probably fly, new research suggests)

"Archaeopteryx lithographica, Archaeopterygidae, Replica of London specimen; Staatliches Museum für Naturkunde Karlsruhe, Germany" (Photo: H. Zell via Wikimedia Commons)

"For decades the late-Jurassic Dino-bird Archaeopteryx stumped paleontologists. 'Was the 150-million-year old bird-dinosaur ground-dwelling?' 'Did it glide or even fly?' Now they may have some answers…. According to the study published in the scientific journal *Nature Communications*, the Archaeopteryx's bone structure is similar to those of 'Volant birds, particularly those occasionally (utilizing) short-distance flapping'; they likened it to that of pheasants 'that occasionally use active flight to cross barriers or dodge predators.' Because of its differences from modern-day birds, more analysis is needed to figure out exactly how it used its wings." [92]

---

[92] Chris Ciacca, "150M year-old dinosaur could probably fly, new research suggests," Fox

Also:

- "Major Evolutionary Blunders: The Imaginary Archaeoraptor"[93]
- "The Enotes Evolution Hoax: Is Micro Raptor a Transitional Fossil? NO."[94]
- "Bye-Bye Birdie: New Look at *Archaeopteryx* Shows It Was More Dinosaur Than Bird"[95]
- "Archaeopteryx, Archaeoraptor, and the "Dinosaurs-to-Birds" Theory"[96]

Will the Evolutionists Ever Give Up?

Horse evolution fraud:

"In 1841, the earliest so-called 'horse' fossil was discovered in clay around London. The scientist who unearthed it, Richard Owen, found a complete skull that looked like a fox's head with multiple back-teeth as in hoofed animals.... An American fossil expert, O.C. Marsh and famous evolutionist, Thomas Huxley ..." produced a schematic diagram which attempted to show the various

News, March 13, 2018, https://www.foxnews.com/science/150m-year-old-dinosaur-could-probably-fly-new-research-suggests.

Video: http://www.foxnews.com/science/2018/03/13/150m-year-old-dinosaur-could-probably-fly-new-research-suggests.html

93   Randy J. Guliuzza, P.E., M.D., "Major Evolutionary Blunders: The Imaginary Archaeoraptor," August 31, 2016, https://www.icr.org/article/major-evolutionary-blunders-imaginary/.

94   Chosenbygrace, "The Enotes Evolution Hoax, Is Micro Raptor a Transitional Fossil? NO." Eternian, November 18, 2010, https://eternian.wordpress.com/tag/wikipedia-archaeoraptor/.

95   Katherin Harmon, "Bye-Bye Birdie: New Look at *Archaeopteryx* Shows It Was More Dinosaur Than Bird," October 9, 2009, https://www.scientificamerican.com/article/archaeopteryx-dinosaur-bird/.

96   Bert Thompson, Ph.D. and Brad Harrub, Ph.D., "Archaeopteryx, Archaeoraptor, and the 'Dinosaurs-to-Birds' Theory—[Part 1]," accessed November 8, 2018, http://www.apologeticspress.org/apPubPage.aspx?pub=1&issue=1205.

stages of the evolution of the modern horse. Although a fake, it found its way into many publications and textbooks. This is what we see in school textbooks today.[97]

Flipperpithecus:

"A 'five million'-year-old piece of bone [called 'flipperpithecus'] that was thought to be a collarbone of a human creature is actually part of a dolphin rib . . . The problem with a lot of anthropologists is that they want so much to find a hominid that any scrap of bone becomes a hominid bone."[98]

"Scientists who go about teaching that evolution is a fact of life are great con-men, and the story they are telling may be the greatest hoax ever. In explaining evolution, we do not have one iota of fact." [95]

(Dr. T.N. Tahmisian (Atomic Energy Commission, USA) in "The Fresno Bee," August 20, 1959.)

2.7   Emergence of the Universe and the Solar System

Let's look at Dr. Duane Gish's take on the emergence of the universe and the solar system, (I).

<u>Creation Model</u>: The universe and the solar system were suddenly created.

---

[97]   Peter Hastie, "Evolution Frauds," Evolution Is Not Science, 1996, https://evolutionisnt science.wordpress.com/evolution-frauds/.

[98]   Conservapedia, "Evolution and Cases of Fraud, Hoaxes and Speculation," last modified September 26, 2018, https://www.conservapedia.com/index.php?title=Evolution_and_Cases_of_Fraud,_Hoaxes_and_Speculation.

[99]   N.J. Mitchell, *Evolution and the Emperor's New Clothes* (Roydon, 1983), title page.

Evolution Model: The universe and the solar system emerged by naturalistic processes.

The Creation View: The "Big-Bang" theory of the origin of the universe contradicts much physical evidence and seemingly can only be accepted by faith. The universe has "obvious manifestations of an ordered, structured plan or design." Similarly, the electron is materially inconceivable and yet it is so perfectly known through its effects, **yet a "strange rationale makes some physicists accept the inconceivable electrons as real while refusing to accept the reality of a Designer."** http://www.icr.org/article/summary-scientific-evidence-for-creation/ (I)

Distant Starlight as an Argument against a Young Earth Universe

You probably heard about and contemplated distant starlight as an argument against a young universe. The argument goes something like this: (1) there are galaxies that are so far away it would take light from their stars billions of years to get from there to here; (2) we can see these galaxies, so their starlight has already arrived here; and (3) the universe must be at least billions of years old—much older than the 6,000 or so years indicated in the Bible.

This is a complex situation, and even Albert Einstein (among others) has offered explanations. Dr. Jason Lisle, of Answers in Genesis—*The New Answers Book 1*—has covered the subject, and some of it is excerpted below[100]:

> God made our eyes to accurately probe the real universe; so we
> can trust that the events that we see in space really happened. For
> this reason, most creation *scientists* believe that "light created

---

[100] Dr. Jason Lisle, "Chapter 19: Does Distant Starlight Prove the Universe Is Old?" Answers in Genesis, December 13, 2007, https://answersingenesis.org/astronomy/starlight/does-distant-starlight-prove-the-universe-is-old/. Used by permission.

in-transit" is not the best way to respond to the distant starlight argument. Let me suggest that the answer to the distant starlight lies in some of the unstated assumptions that secular astronomers make, such as:

1. *The Constancy of the Speed of Light*
2. *The Assumption of Rigidity of Time*
3. *The Assumptions of Synchronization*
4. *The Assumption of Naturalism*

Many of these assumptions are questionable. Do we know that light has always propagated at today's speed? Perhaps this is reasonable, but can we be absolutely certain, particularly during Creation Week when God was acting in a supernatural way? Can we be certain that the Bible is using "cosmic universal time" rather than the more common "cosmic local time" in which light reaches earth instantly?

We know that the rate at which time flows is not rigid. And although secular astronomers are well aware that time is relative, they assume *that this effect is (and has always been) negligible, but can we be certain that this is so? And since stars were made during Creation Week when God was* supernaturally *creating, how do we know for certain that distant starlight has arrived on earth by entirely* natural *means? Furthermore, when Big Bang supporters use distant starlight to argue against biblical creation, they are using a self-refuting argument since the Big Bang has a light travel-time problem of its own. When we consider all of the above, we see that distant starlight has never been a legitimate argument against the biblical timescale of a few thousand years.*

What About the Planets that Always Orbit the Sun?

Walt Brown, in his book, *In the Beginning*, states the evolutionist's problems:

> *Scientists (who don't accept the account of the Creation) can't explain the creation of the earth and its planets. Their view—'They formed from a cloud of swirling dust.'*
>
> *In laymen's terms (to name a few problems), why are all the planets differing in composition and color; differing in distance from the sun; differing in size; differing in their spin axis or tilt axis; differing in their number of moons?*
>
> *In short, each planet is unique. Similarities that would be expected if planets <u>evolved</u> from the same swirling dust are seldom found.*[101]

More Questions

And then there is the problem of what is a planet and how many are there that orbit our sun? It seems the scientists are undecided and still have a lot to learn. As Marina Koren wrote on October 2, 2018, there is a growing case for an elusive ninth planet. I quote the first paragraph of her article:

> **"Astronomy has really wreaked some havoc on science textbooks over the years, particularly when it comes to cataloging the solar system. For most of the 20th century, there were nine planets, taught to our schoolchildren with the help of quirky mnemonics like My Very Excellent Mother Just Served Us Nine Pizzas. Then, in 2006, the Pizzas were dropped; a set of astronomers determined that Pluto was better classified as a dwarf planet than as a full-fledged one. And now, after more than a decade of relative peace, astronomers wish to add a *new***

---

[101] Brown, *In the Beginning,* 24.

ninth planet, upending humanity's understanding of our solar system, not to mention the current school curriculum.[102]

To Close

Dr. Jonathan Wells, with two PhDs in microbiology, has this to say:

"Darwinists have been unable to refute intelligent design with evidence, so they rely on a self-serving definition of science that excludes it from serious consideration."[103]

Also, agnostic scientist Robert Jastrow, founder of the Goddard Institute of Space Studies, writes about the implication of scientific discoveries. The following are three of his quotes:

"Now we see how the astronomical evidence supports the biblical view of the origin of the world. The details differ, but the essential elements in the astronomical and biblical accounts of Genesis are the same: the chain of events leading to man commenced suddenly and sharply at a definite moment in time, in a flash of light and energy."

"It is my view that these circumstances indicate the universe was created for man to live in."

"Scientists have no proof that life was not the result of an act of creation."[104]

---

[102] Marina Koren, "The Growing Case for an Elusive Ninth Planet," *The Atlantic*, October 2, 2018, https://www.theatlantic.com/science/archive/2018/10/search-planet-nine-solar-system/571831/.

[103] Dr. Jonathan Wells, *The Politically Incorrect Guide to Darwinism and Intelligent Design* (Washington DC: Regnery Publishing, 2006), 131.

[104] Inspiring Quotes, "Robert Jastrow Quotes and Sayings - Page 1," accessed November 8, 2018, https://www.inspiringquotes.us/author/7543-robert-jastrow.

Creationist Views:

Since 1982, between 40% and 50% of adults in the United States say they hold the view that "God created humans in their present form at one time within the last 10,000 years" when Gallup asked for their views on the origin and development of human beings. A 2011 Gallup survey reports that 30% of US adults say they interpret the Bible literally. These beliefs are often contradictory. A 2009 poll by Harris Interactive found that 39% of Americans agreed with the statement that "God created the universe, the earth, the sun, moon, stars, plants, animals, and the first two people within the past 10,000 years," yet only 18% of those same Americans agreed with the statement "The earth is less than 10,000 years old."[105]

These statistics are discouraging, so a look at the situation and what's being taught to our children in the public schools might be in order.

---

[105] Wikipedia. 2018. "Young Earth creationism." Article. Last modified November 8, 2018. https://en.wikipedia.org/wiki/Young_Earth_creationism

Now – A Summary of the Situation

Evolution Is a Religion – Not Science!

E volutionists claim that evolution is a scientific fact, but they almost always lose scientific debates with creationist scientists. Accordingly, most evolutionists now decline opportunities for scientific debates, preferring instead to make unilateral attacks on creationists. The fact is that evolutionists believe in evolution because they *want* to. It is their desire at all costs to explain the origin of everything without a Creator. Evolutionism is thus intrinsically an atheistic religion.[106]

"Evolution is a Religion"

Sir Julian Huxley, the primary architect of modern neo-Darwinism, called evolution a "**religion without revelation**" and wrote a book with that title (second edition, 1957).

---

[106] Henry M. Morris, Ph.D., "Evolution Is Religion—Not Science," Institute for Creation Research, February 1, 2001, https://www.icr.org/article/455/.

The Faith and Religion of Evolutionists Explained

Mary Midgley wrote a book, *Evolution as a Religion*, and in it she wrote, "It is time to draw together the threads of this discussion. The myths and dramas we have been considering are various. They do not express a single system but a loose conglomerate of moods, attitudes, and beliefs. What they have in common is, first, that **they center on the theme of evolution**. Second, that while still using official scientific language about the theme, **they are quite contrary to currently accepted scientific doctrines** about it. Third, that they are powerfully emotive and sustaining. They **are so shaped as to provide their adherents with a lively faith** which can be an important element in the meaning of their lives.

Though they do not contain what for our culture are the central marks of a religion—belief in a personal deity and the explicit worship that goes with it—**they seem to have grown up in the response to needs which form some part of the group to which those giving rise to the religious belong**. The tone in which they are expressed makes it impossible to dismiss them as mere accidental factual errors or formal survivals from obsolete doctrines."[107]

And then there was the atheist Michael Ruse

Ardent Darwinian atheist Michael Ruse has also acknowledged that evolution is their religion. Here is what the professor of philosophy, Florida State University, had to say:

> *"Evolution is promoted by its practitioners as more than mere science. Evolution is promulgated as an ideology, a secular religion—a full-fledged alternative to Christianity, with meaning and morality. I am an ardent evolutionist and an ex-Christian,*

---

[107] Mary Midgley, *Evolution as a Religion* (Oxon, UK: Routledge, 2002), 155–156.

but I must admit that in this one complaint—and Mr. Gish (Duane T. Gish the Creation Scientist) is but one of many to make it—the literalists are absolutely right. Evolution is a religion. This was true of evolution in the beginning, and it is true of evolution still today."[108]

What Does the US Constitution Have to Say ... About Religion?

*Congress shall make no law respecting the **establishment of religion**, or prohibiting the free exercise thereof.*

Congress shall make no law establishing one religion sect or society in preference to others.

It prohibits Congress from legislating to establish a national religion.

*It is not allowable per the **establishment clause** for the "coercing" of individuals into acting contrary to their religious beliefs.*

One test of the courts is—does it create excessive entanglement with religion?[109]

Let's Now Step Back and Read Some Definitions of "Religion"

- *A specific fundamental set of beliefs and practices generally agreed upon by a number of persons or sects.*
- *Something one believes in and follows devotedly; a point or matter of ethics or conscience.*[110]

---

[108] Ruse, "Is Darwinism a Religion?"

[109] The Heritage Foundation, "The Heritage Guide to The Constitution," accessed November 8, 2018, https://www.heritage.org/constitution/#!/.

[110] Dictionary.com Unabridged, "Religion," accessed November 8, 2018, https://www.

- *Any specific system of belief, worship, or conduct that prescribes certain responses to the existence (or nonexistence) and character of God.*
- *Atheism is called religion, but the belief denies any power other than man.*[111]

Religion as Taught in Our Public Schools

Congress is allowing (promulgation) of the religion of evolution as a national religion in so far as it is forced on the population of students in our public schools. The students are being "coerced" to undergo the teaching of evolution. "Separation of Church and State" is applied in the model of Creation as "religion" and, therefore, not allowable. **But the model of evolution, which is not scientific but religious, is unfairly allowed in public schools. A dual standard!**

Could we be coercing some class of people (such as Christians) to act contrary to their beliefs when we subject them to (only) the evolution model—and do not allow the offering of the Creation model alongside it in science classes?

The Takeaway Here

1. **The Christian cause is being hurt by the teaching of evolution (and only evolution) in the public schools. As Will Provine says, "Belief in modern evolution makes atheists out of people."**[112]

---

dictionary.com/browse/religion.

[111] All About Religion, "Definition of Religion," accessed November 8, 2018, https://www.allaboutreligion.org/definition-of-religion-faq.htm.

[112] https://creation.com/evolution-makes-atheists-out-of-people

2. The "Establishment Clause" should prohibit the nonscientific religion of Evolution as much as it prohibits the scientific religion of Creation.

3. A powerful legal case may be made for the allowance of the teaching of the scientific aspects of the Creation model beside the scientific aspects of the Evolution model in our public schools.

THE ACTION PLAN

What's Being Taught Now in the Public Schools?

In this book, the scientists get their chance to speak about the Biblical Creation, and as Charles Colson and Walt Brown infer, belief in the Biblical Creation—hence the Christian worldview—most likely would bring about improved results socially for our population. Therefore, most believe that public schools allowing the teaching of Creation would be a positive thing. However, to see the situation, note as of this time there are only two states, Tennessee and Louisiana, that allow public schools to teach Creationism. This is a disturbing situation although there are also some charter schools, mostly in Texas, and private schools that allow Creation teaching.[113]

For the most part, it appears that the science of Creationism is not taught in public schools.

---

[113] Chris Kirk, "Map: Publicly Funded Schools That Are Allowed to Teach Creationism," Slate, January 26, 2014, http://www.slate.com/articles/health_and_science/science/2014/01/creationism_in_public_schools_mapped_where_tax_money_supports_alternatives.html.

The ACLU has been a strong advocate—in most legal cases—to keep Creationism teaching out of the public schools. They bring forth the argument:

> *It is one of the fundamental principles of the Supreme Court's Establishment Clause jurisprudence that the Constitution forbids not only state practices that "aid one religion ... or prefer one religion over another," but also those practices that "aid all religions" and thus endorse or prefer religion over non-religion."*[114]

This argument most often wins the court case.

However, as noted above, Tennessee and Louisiana (with Republican governors and Conservative legislators), have passed **"Science Education Acts" which allows use of Creationism material.** For instance, **in Louisiana,**

> **The act allows public school teachers to use supplemental materials in the science classroom which are critical of theories such as the theory of evolution and global warming.** *Proponents of the law state that it is meant to promote critical thinking and improve education. State Senator Ben Nevers said the law is intended to allow educators to create an environment that "promotes critical thinking skills, logical analysis, and open and objective discussions of scientific theories such as evolution, the origins of life, global warming, and human cloning."*[115]

Note: there is no mention of the Bible.

---

[114] ACLU, "The Establishment Clause and the Schools: A Legal Bulletin," American Civil Rights Union, accessed November 8, 2018, https://www.aclu.org/other/establishment-clause-and-schools-legal-bulletin.

[115] Wikipedia, "Louisiana Science Education Act," last modified June 3, 2018, https://en.wikipedia.org/wiki/Louisiana_Science_Education_Act.

In Tennessee, in 2012,

> The Senate voted 24-8 for SB 893, which would allow teachers to help students "understand, analyze, critique and review in an objective manner the scientific strengths and scientific weaknesses of existing scientific theories" like "biological evolution, the chemical origin of life, global warming and human cloning" . . . "The idea behind this bill is that students should be encouraged to challenge current scientific thought and theory," Republican state Sen. Bo Watson told *The Tennessean*. Watson is the bill's sponsor."[116]

"Teachers Can Teach Creation Science in the Classroom!"

Dr. Robert L. Simonds, Th.D., president and founder of the National Association of Christian Educators and Citizens for Excellence in Education, P.O. Box 3200, Costa Mesa, CA 92628, wrote a lengthy article, excerpted below:

> *"The U.S. Supreme Court developed a three-prong test in* Lemon v. Kurtzas *to when government involvement in **religious activity does not violate the establishment clause: (1) The activity must have a secular purpose; (2) its primary effect must be neither to advance nor inhibit religion; (3) it must not constitute excessive entanglement of government with religion.***"[117]

---

[116] "Tennessee Science Bill Allowing Discussion Of Creationism In Schools Passes State Senate," *Huffington Post*, March 20, 2012, https://www.huffingtonpost.com/2012/03/20/tennessee-science-bill-al_n_1368261.html.

[117] Robert L. Simonds, "Teachers Can Teach Creation Science in the Classroom," Institute for Creation Research, October 1, 1989, https://www.icr.org/article/teachers-can-teach-creation-science-classroom/.

The David C. Gibbs III law firm in their book, *Making Sense of Religion in America's Public Schools*, summarized the Supreme Court view, as in Edwards vs. Aguillard, 482 U.S. 96 (1987, as follows:

> **"The United States Supreme Court has never mandated that Darwinism be taught as fact rather than theory; nor have judges ever prohibited teachers from teaching scientific evidence disproving evolution to public school students. In fact, while the Supreme Court said in this case that Creation was a religion, the Court at the same time indicated its approval of a science curriculum that would teach much more than evolution."** [118]
>
> . . . .

> *"No new laws are necessary; there is no possible violation of so-called separation of church and state, since no religious teaching is involved.*

> *The recent Texas "Proclamation 66" requires all textbooks to:*

> 1. *Present more than one theory of evolution (this shows up the internal divisions on evolution dogma);*
> 2. *Examine alternative scientific evidence and ideas on origins (this forces the discussion of scientific creationism both as an idea and a theory);*
> 3. *Present evidence to test, verify, modify, or refute each theory of evolution discussed;*
> 4. *Present any other reliable scientific theories of origins.*

> *It does seem that the educational pendulum could be swinging back to center. However, the battle is not over, by any means."* [119]

---

[118] David C. Gibbs and Barbara J. Weller, *Making Sense of Religion in America's Pubic Schools* (Largo, FL: The National Center for Life and Liberty, 2013), 165.

[119] Simonds, "Teachers Can Teach Creation Science in the Classroom."

The Appropriate Role of Religion in the Public School Curriculum

A consensus has emerged among diverse religions and educational groups about the appropriate role for religion in the public school curriculum. Both liberal and conservative legal and educational groups who want to avoid any religious indoctrination in public schools agree on the following principles regarding the appropriate role for religion in the public school curriculum:

The school's approach to religion is *academic,* not *devotional.*

The school may strive for student *awareness* of religions, but should press for student *acceptance* of any religion.

The school may sponsor *study* about religion, but may not sponsor the *practice* of religion.

The school may *expose* students to a diversity of religious views, but may not *impose, discourage, or encourage* any particular view.

The school may *educate* about all religions, but may not *promote or denigrate* any religion.

The school may *inform* students about various beliefs, but should not seek to *conform* them to a particular belief.[120]

States Where Action Is Taking Place and/or Are Ready for Action

There are thirty-three states with Republican governors;[121] hence, *the iron is hot* for action. Further, there are eleven states with creation organiza-

---

[120] Gibbs and Weller, *Making Sense of Religion in America's Pubic Schools,* 125.

[121] Wikipedia, "List of current United States governors," last modified November 8, 2018, https://en.wikipedia.org/wiki/List_of_current_United_States_governors.

tions within the state. **Why not contact these organizations and start a conversation with your legislators**.

Alabama	–	Apologetics Press
Arizona	–	Creation Research Society
Florida	–	Creation Studies Institute, Creation Science Evangelism, The International Association for Creation
Georgia	–	Creation Ministries International, Atlanta Creation Group
Idaho	–	4th Day Alliance
Indiana	–	Indiana Creation Science Association, Creation Liberty Evangelism
Kansas	–	Creation Science Association for Mid America
Kentucky	–	Answers in Genesis
South Carolina	–	Creation Studies Group, Genesis Science Mission
Tennessee	–	Dan Rives Ministries
Texas	–	Institute for Creation Research, Creation Science League

Introducing Creationism into Public Schools

In 1974, Dr. Henry M. Morris, in an article[122], reminded all that we need to get involved, including:

1. Creationist Scientists
2. School Administrators
3. Teachers
4. Pastors
5. Scientists in General
6. Parents and Other People
7. Students

---

[122] Henry M. Morris, Ph.D., "Introducing Creationism into Public Schools," Institute for Creation Research, November 1, 1974, https://www.icr.org/article/66/.

Please access his article and find more about what you can do:
https://www.icr.org/article/66/.

Legislation and Speaking with a Lawyer

Not all attempts to influence how evolution is taught have failed. Alabama, Minnesota, Missouri, Pennsylvania, South Carolina, and Texas all require in their science standards that students "critically analyze key aspects of evolutionary theory." In addition, Louisiana and Mississippi have legislation allowing teachers and students to discuss scientific evidence critical of evolution. Citizens of these named states should check with the school boards to see if these positive actions are actually taking place to the benefit of all students.

Litigation on this issue continues at every level. Whatever your position on the issue, seek an experienced education attorney. One such source is the National Center for Life and Liberty (NCLL). www.NCLL.org. The law firm founded by David Gibbs III now has over a dozen legal professionals and has argued several cases that have defined the religious landscape in America. The NCLL is well equipped to assist more than 3,000 churches in a given year, with over 200 active cases at any given time. They have offered to assist in our quest, so consider making contact. NCLL offices are in Largo, FL; Dallas, TX; El Centro, CA; Winston-Salem, NC; Washington, DC; and Cleveland, OH. Phone 727-362-3700 and 888-233-NCLL (6255)

Creation vs. Evolutionism – Where We Stand Today

As you have read through these pages, you may be impressed by the revelation of the great number of scientists with PhDs who believe in Creation rather than evolution.

And it may also be shocking to realize that polls tell us that we are a Christian nation, because many want to tell us that we are not a Christian nation anymore—or at least we should not be acting that way. Looking back in time, in early days, schools and universities taught the Christian doctrine—from the Bible. Now, those with other worldviews seem to have taken over, and year after year their cause has gained ground, especially in our public schools.

The National Science Teachers Association is greatly opposed to teaching anything on Creationism as a science in public schools,[123] as is the Association for Science Teacher Education, the National Association of Biology Teachers, the American Anthropological Association, the American Science Institute, the Geological Society of America, the American Geophysical Union, and the National Center for Science Education (NCSE).[124]

Legislation Put Forward to Get Creationism Taught in the Public Schools

Against this bleak backdrop, and the apparent apathy of the overall Christian population through the years, a number of courageous state legislators have tried (in vain) to put forth bills to allow Creationism to be covered alongside evolution in our public schools. Over the period of 2004–2015, there were approximately fifty-five bills put forward.

This was the result. In Louisiana, there was a win for "Academic Freedom" in 2008, and in Tennessee in 2011, there was a win that "protects a teacher from discipline for teaching scientific subjects in an objective manner." **In all the rest, the bills were tabled or defeated![125]**

---

[123] Wikipedia, "Creation and evolution in public education in the United States," last modified July 12, 2018, https://en.wikipedia.org/wiki/Creation_and_evolution_in_public_education_in_the_United_States#Louisiana.

[124] National Center for Science Education, "Evolution," accessed November 8, 2018, https://ncse.com/node/16774.

[125] NCSE Staff, "Chronology of 'Academic Freedom Bills'," National Center for Science Education, February 7, 2013, https://ncse.com/creationism/general/chronology-academic-freedom-bills.

All this obstructionism is in the face of the positive Christian world-view—for the good. As a case in point, after the senseless shooting on June 17, 2015, at the Emanuel African Methodist Church in Charleston, South Carolina, the families of those killed took a particularly Christian attitude—to the amazement of many. From the Charleston Police Department, it was stated, **"I've never seen the multitude of victims as forgiving as this."** Indeed, the Christian worldview is beneficial to our society. Once again, as Charles Colson states in his book *A Dance with Deception*:

The lesson of history is clear: When Christian belief is strong, the crime rate falls; when Christian belief weakens, the crime rate climbs. Widespread religious belief creates a shared social ethic that acts as a restraint on the dark side of human nature.[126]

To save our country by saving our kids, what we need most could be called "Public Safety Bills" or "Anti-Crime Bills" as opposed to the evolutionist's obstructionism.

"Thank you everyone for signing the petition."

Yes, the battle for legislation is being lost because the atheist minority are more forceful, more aggressive, and louder. They are well-organized and **often put forth petitions to the school boards and state legislators that win them the victory.** One petition put together by Eduardo Pazos, using petition model *Change.org*, was titled, "Stop FL anti-evolution bill (SB 1854)." It was submitted to the Florida State House with 284 signers in July 2011. The last statement by Eduardo Pazos was: "The bill is dead. Thank you everyone for signing the petition."[127]

---

126 Colson, *A Dance with Deception*, 190.

127 Eduardo Pazos, "Stop FL anti-evolution education bill (SB 1854)," Change.org, accessed November 8, 2018, https://www.change.org/p/stop-fl-anti-evolution-education-bill-sb-1854.

It's Now Time for US (The Silent Majority) To Speak Out

It is understandable if the courageous legislators who led the fight with the previous unsuccessful bills are now "burned out" and *discouraged*. **But we are in the majority, so let's take heart!**

In 2006, a poll conducted by Zogby International commissioned by the Discovery Institute found that most voters surveyed chose the option that *"biology teachers should teach Darwin's Theory of evolution, but also the scientific evidence against it"* (more than three to one). Approximately seven in ten (69%) sided with this view.[128]

In contrast, one in five (21%) chose the other option given that "biology teachers should teach only Darwin's Theory of Evolution and the scientific evidence that supports it." Only one in ten was "not sure" (10%).

The Zogby Poll Results as the Percent of the Population

1. Teach Darwin's theory of Evolution only   21%
2. Teach Evolution plus **scientific evidence against it**   69%
3. Not sure   10%
             100%

Step-by-Step Guidelines for Taking Action in Your State

The road ahead for our cause is not an easy one, but it is worth it. Dr. Paul Ackerman and Bob Williams recorded their long battle to improve the 1999 Kansas curriculum, and an important summary they gave was a

---

[128] Free Science Today, "In Zogby Poll, 69% Favor Teaching Evidence for and Against Darwin's Theory," accessed November 8, 2018. https://freescience.today/2006/03/07/in-zogby-poll-69-favor-teaching-evidence-for-and-against-darwins-theory/. Used by permission.

twenty point *words to the wise* 'Step-by-Step Principles and Guidelines for Taking Action in Your State.'[129] It is well worth a read.

Let's All Now Sign the Discovery Institute's 'Academic Freedom Petition'

Let's start with something about the Discovery Institute and then on to their 'Academic Freedom Petition." Rather than offering explanations of how the universe and humans began, proponents of intelligent design (a) state that life arose through a purposeful plan by a divine being and (b) seek to expose flaws in specific applications of Darwinian theory. Thus, the Discovery Institute's position on teaching about human beginnings is that—'examination of evidence and critical thinking are the hallmarks of good science education ... it follows that students should learn about the scientific data that supports Darwin's Theory of Evolution, as well as the data that goes against the theory and which continues to puzzle scientists.... Our recommendation is that students receive a full and fair disclosure of the facts surrounding Darwin's theory and that the leading scientific criticisms of the theory not be censored from classroom discussion.'[130] (Discovery Institute staff, 2004).

This has led to the Discovery Institute's 'Academic Freedom Petition,' and by signing the petition, you can join the many who have taken action by expressing their opinion. To sign the petition, you can go to https://freescience.today/petition/. Also, please visit Appendix H to learn more about the petition.

---

[129] Dr. Paul Ackerman and Bob Williams, *Kansas Tornado: The 1999 Science Curriculum Standards Battle* (Dallas: Institute for Creation Research, 1999), 59-62.

[130] Thomas, *God in the Classroom: Religion and America's Public Schools*, p. 65.

Finally

Yes, it's now time for the silent majority to finally come forward and lead the fight—with "grassroots campaigns" and a series of information presentations and actions as needed.

An information campaign led by church pastors and members, Creation scientist groups, legal firms, school boards, and concerned citizens could make an important difference if:

1. we all read about the subject and started the conversation;
2. we gave our views to the school boards and legislators who are the decision makers; and
3. we initiate needed petitions in support of needed legislation.

In addition, or as an alternative to success with the public schools, it is suggested church pastors take steps to create their own church schools or promote other local Christian schools to their members. Also, concerned families can start their own home schooling program for their children.

To Save Our Country by Saving Our Kids

"And the gospel of the kingdom shall be preached in all the world for a witness unto all nations; and then shall the end come"
Matthew 24:14 (KJV)

Recent (active and published) Believers in Biblical Creation who Possess a Doctorate in a Science Related Field

Also of interest: There is a new list of more than 1,000 doctoral scientist names, world-wide, who share their own doubts about Darwinian Evolution. Please see: www.dissentfromdarwin.org.

The following is a list of "some scientists alive today* who accept the biblical account of creation."[131]

Note: Individuals below—223 believers in the Biblical Creation—possess an earned doctorate in a field of science or (for the rare person lacking a PhD) high-level research achievements or academic status.

---

[131] Creation Ministries International, "Some scientists alive today* who accept the biblical account of creation."

Note: Individuals on this list possess an earned doctorate in a field of science, or (for the rare person lacking a PhD) high-level research achievements or academic status.

- Dr. Paul Ackerman, Assistant Professor of Psychology, Wichita State University.
- Dr. E. Theo Agard, Medical Physics
- Dr. James Allan, Genetics
- Dr. John Ashton, Chemistry, Food technology
- Dr. Steve Austin, Geology
- Dr. S.E. Aw, Biochemistry
- Dr. Geoff Barnard, Immunology
- Dr. Don Batten, Plant Physiology
- Dr. Donald Baumann, Solid State Physics, Professor of Biology and Chemistry, Cedarville University
- Dr. John Baumgardner, Electrical Engineering, Space Physicist, Geophysicist, Expert In Supercomputer Modeling of Plate Tectonics
- Dr. Élizabeth Beauchesne, Biomedical Sciences.
- Dr. Jerry Bergman, Psychology, Human Biology/Physiology
- Dr. Kimberly Berrine, Microbiology and Immunology
- Prof. Vladimir Betina, Microbiology, Biochemistry and Biology
- Dr. Markus Blietz, Astrophysicist
- Dr. Raymond G. Bohlin, Biology
- Dr. Andrew Bosanquet, Biology, Microbiology
- Dr. Edward A. Boudreaux, Theoretical Chemistry
- Dr. David Boylan, Chemical Engineering
- Dr. Bernard Brandstater, Anesthesiology
- Prof. Stuart Burgess, Engineering and Biomimetics, Professor of Design and Nature, Head of Department, Mechanical Engineering, University of Bristol (UK)
- Prof. Linn E. Carothers, Associate Professor of Statistics
- Dr. Ben Carson, Professor and Chief of Pediatric Neurosurgery

at Johns Hopkins University. He has 51 honorary doctorates, including from Yale and Columbia Universities.

- Dr. Robert W. Carter, Marine Biology
- Dr. David Catchpoole, Plant Physiology (read his story)
- Prof. Sung-Do Cha, Physics
- Dr. Eugene F. Chaffin, Professor of Physics
- Dr. Ainsley Chalmers, Biochemist, Medical Researcher
- Dr. Choong-Kuk Chang, Genetic Engineering
- Prof. Jeun-Sik Chang, Aeronautical Engineering
- Dr. Xidong Chen, Solid State Physics, Assistant Professor of Physics, Cedarville University
- Dr. Donald Chittick, Physical Chemistry
- Prof. Chung-Il Cho, Biology Education
- Dr. John M. Cimbala, Mechanical Engineering
- Dr. Harold Coffin, Paleontology
- Dr. Bob Compton, DVM, PhD
- Dr. Ken Cumming, Biology
- Dr. Malcolm Cutchins, Aerospace Engineering
- Dr. Lionel Dahmer, Analytical Chemistry
- Dr. Raymond V. Damadian, M.D., Pioneer of Magnetic Resonance Imaging
- Dr. Chris Darnbrough, Biochemistry
- Dr. Nancy M. Darrall, Botany
- Dr. Bryan Dawson, Mathematics
- Dr. Douglas Dean, Biological Chemistry
- Prof. Stephen W. Deckard, Assistant Professor of Education
- Dr. David A. DeWitt, Biology, Biochemistry, Neuroscience
- Dr. Don DeYoung, Astronomy, Atmospheric Physics
- Dr. Geoff Downes, Plant Physiology
- Dr. Ted Driggers, Operations research
- Robert H. Eckel, Medical Research (more than 80 research papers)
- Dr. André Eggen, Genetics

- Dr. Leroy Eimers, Atmospheric Science, Professor of Physics and Mathematics, Cedarville University
- Dr. Dudley Eirich, Molecular Biologist
- Prof. Dennis L. Englin, Professor of Geophysics
- Prof. Danny Faulkner, Astronomy
- Dr. Dennis Flentge, Physical Chemistry, Professor of Chemistry and Chair of the Department of Science and Mathematics, Cedarville University
- Prof. Carl B. Fliermans, Professor of Biology
- Prof. Dwain L. Ford, Organic Chemistry
- Prof. Robert H. Franks, Associate Professor of Biology
- Dr. Kenneth W. Funk, Organic Chemistry; Biologically Active Peptide Synthesis.
- Dr. Alan Galbraith, Watershed Science
- Dr. Roger G. Gallop, P.G., Geology
- Dr. Robert Gentry, Physics
- Dr. Maciej Giertych, Genetics
- Dr. Werner Gitt, Information Science
- Dr. Steven Gollmer, Atmospheric Science, Professor of Physics, Cedarville University
- Dr. D.B. Gower, Biochemistry
- Dr. Stephen Grocott, Industrial Chemistry
- Dr. Donald Hamann, Food Science
- Dr. Barry Harker, Philosophy
- Dr. Charles W. Harrison, Applied Physics, Electromagnetics
- Dr. John Hartnett, Physics and Cosmology
- Dr. Mark Harwood, Satellite Communications
- Dr. Joe Havel, Botanist, Silviculture, Ecophysiology
- Dr. George Hawke, Environmental Science
- Dr. Steven Hayes, Nuclear Science
- Dr. Margaret Helder, Science Editor, Botany
- Dr. Larry Helmick, Organic Chemistry, Professor of Chemistry, Cedarville University

- Dr. Harold R. Henry, Engineering
- Dr. Dewey Hodges, Professor of Aerospace Engineering
- Dr. Joseph Henson, Entomology
- Dr. Jonathan Henry, Chemical Engineering, Astronomy
- Dr. Robert A. Herrmann, Professor of Mathematics, US Naval Academy
- Dr. Kelly Hollowell, Molecular and Cellular Pharmacology
- Dr. Ed Holroyd, III, Atmospheric Science
- Dr. Bob Hosken, Biochemistry
- Dr. George F. Howe, Botany
- Dr. Neil Huber, Physical Anthropology
- Dr. Russell Humphreys, Physics
- Dr. James A. Huggins, Professor and Chair, Department of Biology
- Dr. G. Charles Jackson, Science Education
- Dr. Evan Jamieson, Hydrometallurgy
- Prof. George T. Javor, Biochemistry
- Dr. Pierre Jerlström, Molecular Biology
- Dr. Arthur Jones, Biology
- Dr. Raymond Jones, Agricultural Science
- Dr. Valery Karpounin, Mathematical Sciences, Logic, Formal Logic
- Dr. Dean Kenyon, Biology
- Prof. Gi-Tai Kim, Biology
- Prof. Harriet Kim, Biochemistry
- Prof. Jong-Bai Kim, Biochemistry
- Prof. Jung-Han Kim, Biochemistry
- Prof. Jung-Wook Kim, Environmental Science
- Prof. Kyoung-Rai Kim, Analytical Chemistry
- Prof. Kyoung-Tai Kim, Genetic Engineering
- Prof. Young-Gil Kim, Materials Science
- Prof. Young In Kim, Engineering
- Dr. David King, Astronomy.

- Dr. John W. Klotz, Biology
- Dr. Vladimir F. Kondalenko, Cytology/Cell Pathology
- Dr. Felix Konotey-Ahulu, Physician, Leading Expert on Sickle-Cell Anemia
- Dr. Leonid Korochkin, M.D., Genetics, Molecular Biology, Neurobiology
- Dr. John K.G. Kramer, Biochemistry
- Dr. Johan Kruger, Zoology
- Dr. Wolfgang Kuhn, Biology Researcher and Lecturer
- Dr. Heather Kuruvilla, Plant Physiology, Senior Professor of Biology, Cedarville University
- Prof. Jin-Hyouk Kwon, Physics
- Prof. Myung-Sang Kwon, Immunology
- Dr. Barry Lawrence, Nuclear Engineering
- Dr. Matti Leisola, Biochemistry (esp. of enzymes), D.Sc. in biotechnology, Dean, Faculty of Chemical and Materials Sciences, Aalta University, Finland
- Dr. John G. Leslie, Biochemistry, Molecular Biology, Medicine, Biblical Archaeology
- Prof. Lane P. Lester, Biology, Genetics
- Dr. Jean Lightner, Agriculture, Veterinary science
- Dr. Peter Line, Neuroscience
- Dr. Jason Lisle, Astrophysics
- Dr. Raúl E López, Meteorology
- Dr. Alan Love, Chemistry
- Dr. Gloria Luciani-Torres, Molecular Oncology Researcher (Cancer Biology)
- Dr. Heinz Lycklama, Nuclear Physics and Information Technology
- Dr. Ian Macreadie, Molecular Biology and Microbiology
- Dr. John Marcus, Molecular Biology
- Dr. George Marshall, Opthalmology researcher
- Dr. James Mason, Nuclear physics

- Dr. Ralph Matthews, Radiation Chemistry
- Dr. Mark McClain, Inorganic Chemistry, Associate Professor of Chemistry, Cedarville University
- Dr. John McEwan, Organic Chemistry
- Prof. Andy McIntosh, Combustion Theory, Aerodynamics
- Dr. David Menton, Anatomy
- Dr. Angela Meyer, Plant Physiology
- Dr. John Meyer, Physiology
- Dr. Victor Meyer, Entomology, Environmental Science
- Dr. Douglas Miller, Professor of Chemistry, Cedarville University
- Dr. Robert T. Mitchell, Internal Medicine (specialist)
- Dr. Colin W. Mitchell, Geography
- Dr. Gina Mohammed, Plant physiology
- Dr. John N. Moore, Science Education
- Dr. John D. Morris, Geology
- Dr. Len Morris, Physiology
- Dr. Graeme Mortimer, Geology
- Dr. Stanley A. Mumma, Architectural Engineering
- Dr. Ron Neller, Fluvial Geomorphology
- Prof. Hee-Choon No, Nuclear Engineering
- Dr. Eric Norman, Biomedical science
- Dr. David Oderberg, Philosophy
- Professor Douglas Oliver, Professor of Biology
- Prof. John Oller, Linguistics
- Prof. Chris D. Osborne, Assistant Professor of Biology
- Dr. Charles Pallaghy, Botany
- Dr. Gary E. Parker, Biology, Cognate in Geology (Paleontology)
- Dr. Terry Phipps, Professor of Biology, Cedarville University
- Dr. Jules H. Poirier, Aeronautics, Electronics
- Dr. Georgia Purdom, Molecular Genetics
- Dr. Graeme Quick, Engineering, Former Principal Research Scientist with CSIRO (Australia)

- Dr. Dan Reynolds, Organic Chemistry
- Dr. Chad Rodekohr, Engineering, Physics
- Dr. Jung-Goo Roe, Biology
- Dr. David Rodda, PhD, Population Genetics
- Dr. David Rosevear, Chemistry
- Dr. Marcus Ross, Paleontology
- Dr. Ariel A. Roth, Biology
- Dr. Craig Russell, Soil Science, Plant Nutrition, Ecology
- Dr. Ronald G. Samec, Astronomy
- Dr. John Sanford, Plant Science / Genetics
- Dr. Jonathan D. Sarfati, Physical chemistry / spectroscopy
- Dr. Alicia (Lisa) Schaffner, Associate Professor of Biology, Cedarville University
- Dr. Joachim Scheven Paleontology
- Dr. Ian Scott, Education
- Dr. Saami Shaibani, Forensic Physics
- Dr. Young-Gi Shim, Chemistry
- Prof. Hyun-Kil Shin, Food Science
- Dr. Mikhail Shulgin, Physics
- Dr. Emil Silvestru, Geology/karstology
- Dr. Roger Simpson, Engineering
- Dr. Horace D. ('Skip') Skipper, Professor Emeritus Soil microbiology, College of Agriculture, Forestry and Life Sciences, Clemson University, SC, USA
- Dr. E. Norbert Smith, Zoology
- Dr. Andrew Snelling, Geology
- Prof. Man-Suk Song, Computer Science
- Dr. Timothy G. Standish, Biology
- Prof. James Stark, Assistant Professor of Science Education
- Prof. Brian Stone, Engineer
- Dr. Esther Su, Biochemistry
- Dr. Dennis Sullivan, Biology, Surgery, Chemistry, Professor of Biology, Cedarville University

- Dr. Greg Tate, Plant Pathology
- Dr. Stephen Taylor, Electrical Engineering
- Dr. Larry Thaete, Molecular and Cellular Biology and Pathobiology
- Dr. Ker C. Thomson, Geophysics
- Dr. Michael Todhunter, Forest Genetics
- Dr. Lyudmila Tonkonog, Chemistry/Biochemistry
- Dr. S.H. 'Wally' Tow (Tow Siang Hwa), Retired Chairman of the Department of Obstetrics and Gynecology at the University of Singapore
- Dr. Royal Truman, Organic Chemistry
- Dr. Brandon van der Ventel, Nuclear Scientist
- Dr. Gerald Van Dyke, Ph.D. and Professor Emeritus in Botany, North Carolina State University
- Dr. Larry Vardiman, Atmospheric Science
- Prof. Walter Veith, Zoology
- Dr. Joachim Vetter, Biology
- Dr. Erich Vorpagel, Biochemistry, Molecular Biology; Computational Protein Function
- Dr. Tas Walker, Mechanical Engineering and Geology
- Dr. Jeremy Walter, Mechanical Engineering
- Dr. Keith Wanser, Physics
- Dr. Noel Weeks, Ancient Near-East History (also has B.Sc. in Zoology)
- Dr. Carl Werner, Biologist
- Dr. A.J. Monty White, Chemistry/Gas Kinetics
- Dr. John Whitmore, Geology/Paleontology
- Dr. Kurt Wise, Paleontology
- Dr. Bryant Wood, Archaeology
- Prof. Seoung-Hoon Yang, Physics
- Dr. Thomas (Tong Y.) Yi, Aerospace and Mechanical Engineering
- Dr. Ick-Dong Yoo, Genetics

- Dr. Sung-Hee Yoon, Biology
- Dr. Patrick Young, Chemistry and Materials Science
- Prof. Keun Bae Yu, Geography
- Dr. Daiqing Yuan, Theoretical Physics
- Dr. Henry Zuill, Biology

* Or recently deceased.

Note: Some of those listed may be recently deceased, and some names may have been inadvertently omitted.

Please see also:

1. "Creation & Earth History Museum, Creation Scientists," http://www.creationsd.org/creation-scientists.html
2. "Who's Who in Creation/Evolution," https://christiananswers. net/creation/people/home.html

APPENDIX B

ANCIENT WRITINGS THAT CORROBORATE THE EVENTS OF THE HOLY BIBLE

"Let the debate continue, but let the evidence be admitted. Ever since scientific archaeology started a century and a half ago, the consistent pattern has been this: the hard evidence from the ground has borne out the biblical record again and again—and again. The Bible has nothing to fear from the spade."[132]

Yes! Here are just 8 bits of evidence from the ancients that corroborate the existence of the people and the events that can be read about in the Holy Bible.

---

[132] Maier, "Biblical Archaeology: Factual Evidence to Support the Historicity of the Bible."

Jehoiachin's Ration Tablets
Akkadian
Early Sixth Century BC
Ref. 2 Kings 25:27–30

Jehoiachin's rations tablets date from the sixth century BC and describe the rations set aside for a royal captive identified with Jeconiah, king of Judah. Tablets from

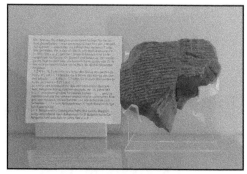

"Jehoiachin's Rations Tablet, Pergamon Museum, Berlin"
Photo: Scallaham via Wikimedia Commons

the royal archives of Nebuchadnezzar king of Babylon were unearthed in the ruins of Babylon that contain food rations paid to captives and craftsmen who lived in and around the city. On one of the tablets, "Ya'u-kinu, king of the land of Yahudu," is mentioned along with his five sons listed as royal princes.[133]

Nabonidus Chronicle
Akkadian
Mid-Sixth Century BC

In spite of the brevity of the Nabonidus Chronicle—the tablet measures about 14 cm (5.5 in.) in breadth at about the widest point and about the same in length—it remains the most complete cuneiform record of the fall of Babylon available. Interestingly, the Chronicle

"The Nabonidus Chronicle" (British Museum)
Photo: ChrisO via Wikimedia Commons

says concerning the night of Babylon's fall: "The army of Cyrus entered Babylon without a battle." This likely means without a general conflict and

---

[133] Wikipedia, "Jehoiachin's Rations Tablets," last modified September 25, 2018, https://en.wikipedia.org/wiki/Jehoiachin%27s_Rations_Tablets.

agrees with the prophecy of Jeremiah that 'the mighty men of Babylon would cease to fight.'—Jer 51:30.[134]

Nebuchadnezzar Chronicle
Akkadian
Early Sixth Century BC
Ref. Daniel 5:29–30

The Nebuchadnezzar Chronicle, also known as (Jerusalem Chronicle), is one of the series of Babylonian Chronicles, and contains a description of the first eleven years of the reign of Nebuchadnezzar II. The tablet details Nebuchadnezzar's military campaigns in the west and has been interpreted to refer to both the Battle of Carchemish and the Siege of Jerusalem (597 BC).[135]

Clay tablet; New Babylonian. Chronicle for years 605-594 BC © The Trustees of the British Museum

Mesha Stele (Moabite Stone)
Moabite
Ninth Century BC
Ref. 2 Kings 3:4

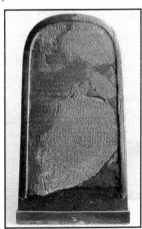

"Last year the French scholar Andre Lemaire reported a related 'House of David' discovery in *Biblical Archaeology Review.* His subject was the Mesha Stele (also known as the Moabite Stone), the most extensive inscription ever recovered from ancient Palestine. Found in

Mesha Stele
Photo: Mbzt 2012 via
Wikimedia Commons

---

[134] Watchtower Bible & Tract Society, "Insight on the Scriptures Volumes 1 & 2," 1998, 459–460, https://wol.jw.org/en/wol/d/r1/lp-e/1200003156.

[135] Wikipedia, "Nebuchadnezzar Chronicle," June 17, 2018, https://en.wikipedia.org/wiki/Nebuchadnezzar_Chronicle.

1868 at the ruins of biblical Dibon and later fractured, the basalt stone wound up in the Louvre, where Lemaire spent seven years studying it. His conclusion: the 'House of David' appears there as well. As with the Tel Dan fragment, this inscription comes from an enemy of Israel boasting of a victory—King Mesha of Moab, who figured in the Bible."[136]

Merneptah Stele
Egyptian
Thirteenth Century BC

The discovery of the Israel Stele is very important in the study of Biblical archaeology. It
is the oldest evidence of Israel in the land of
Canaan in ancient times outside the Bible. The
text on the stone reads: *"Canaan is plundered
with every evil way. Ashkelon is conquered and
brought away captive, Gezer seized, Yanoam
made nonexistent; Israel is wasted, bare of
seed."*—Merneptah Stele[137]

Merneptah Stele (Egyptian
Museum, Cairo)
Photo: Webscribe via
Wikimedia Commons

Sargon Legend
Akkadian
First millennium BC
Ref. Exodus 2

According to the cuneiform inscription known as *The Legend of Sargon*
(his autobiography), he was born the illegitimate son of a "changeling,"
which could refer to a temple priestess of the goddess Inanna (whose
clergy were androgynous) and never knew his father. His mother could

---

[136] Michael D. Lemonick, "Are the Bible Stories True?" *Time Magazine*, December 18, 1995.

[137] Bible History, "The Israel Stela (Merneptah Stele)," accessed November 8, 2018, https://www.bible-history.com/archaeology/egypt/2-israel-stela-bb.html.

not reveal her pregnancy or keep her child, and so placed him in a basket which she then let go on the Euphrates River. She had sealed the basket with tar, and the water carried him safely to where he was later found by a man named Akki who was a gardener for Ur-Zababa, the king of the Sumerian city of Kish.[138]

Clay tablet relating the birth of Sargon of Akkad. Photo: Jastrow via Wikimedia Commons

Atrahasis Epic
Akkadian
Early Second Millennium BC
Ref. Genesis 1–9

The Epic of Atrahasis is the fullest Mesopotamian **account of the Great Flood**, with Atrahasis in **the role of Noah.** Covered in the epic were creation of Man, conditions immediately after the Creation, and events concerning the Flood—the construction of the ark, boarding the ark, and departure.[139]

Cuneiform tablet with the Atrahasis Epic (British Museum) Photo: Jack1956* via Wikimedia Commons

---

[138] Joshua J. Mark, "The Legend of Sargon of Akkad," Ancient History Encyclopedia, August 30, 2014, https://www.ancient.eu/article/746/the-legend-of-sargon-of-akkad/.

[139] Livius, "The Epic of Atrahasis," last modified January 3, 2017, http://www.livius.org/sources/content/anet/104-106-the-epic-of-atrahasis/.

Gilgamesh Epic
Akkadian
Early Second Millennium BC
Ref. Genesis 6–9

"Flood Tablet" (British Museum)
Photo: BabelStone via Wikimedia Commons

"In reality, it was Utnapishtim's flood, told in the eleventh tablet. The council of gods decided to **flood the whole earth** to destroy mankind. But Ea, the god who made man, warned Utnapishtim from Shuruppak, a city on the banks of the Euphrates, that he should build an enormous boat....

Utnapishtim sealed his ark with pitch, took ... his family members [and all kinds of vertebrate animals] plus some other humans. Shamash the sun god showered down loaves of bread and rained down wheat. Then the flood came.... [Later], the ark lodged on Mt. Nisir (or Nimush), almost 500 km (300 miles) from Mt Ararat."[140]

---

[140] Jonathan Sarfati, "Noah's Flood and the Gilgamesh Epic," Creation Ministries International, September 12–17, 2006. https://creation.com/noahs-flood-and-the-gilgamesh-epic.

APPENDIX C

EYEWITNESS ACCOUNTS OF NOAH'S ARK ON MOUNT ARARAT

1800s and 1900s—Jacob Chuchian lived on the south side of Mt. Ararat and visited the site of the Ark often. In that period, a "smooth year" without much snow occurred only every twenty years or so. **Over that time, he gave eyewitness accounts and sketches.**[141]

1908 and 1910—George Hagopian visited the Ark with his uncle, both Armenians: "I remember my uncle took his gun and shot into the side of the Ark, but the bullet wouldn't penetrate. Uncle then pulled the long hunting knife from his belt, and with the heavy handle **he chipped a piece from the side of the Ark.** Then we went down the mountainside."[142]

1916–1917—Czar Nicholas II commissioned two expeditions to the Ark, and photographs were taken. Later, when the Bolsheviks took over, all

---

[141] David W. Balsiger and Charles E. Seller, *Miraculous Messages from Noah's Flood to the End Times* (Alachua, FL: Bridge-Logos, 2008), 219.

[142] B.J. Corbin, *The Explorers of Ararat and The Search for Noah's Ark* (Great Commission Illustrated Books, 1999), 369–3711.

photographs and records were destroyed, but **many on the expeditions had detailed stories to tell.**[143]

1943—Sergeant Ed Davis was taken by a local Iranian to Mount Ararat and the Ark. **"He says there are cages inside as small as your hand and others big enough to hold a family of elephants."**[144]

1945–1946—Air Force Corporal Lester Walton was flying a B-24 with high-tech cameras over Mount Ararat when he inadvertently snapped some shots of Noah's Ark. He recounted that **"a number of those who saw the footage believed this to be the Ark of Noah."**[145]

1974—Navy Lieutenant J G Al Shappell with his F-4 jet fitted with special cameras was sent to photograph a possible Soviet threat on Mount Ararat, a dark box-shaped object of man-made origin. The lieutenant clearly remembers seeing the long boxlike structure and sketched it from memory. **However, the film was turned over to the Air Force and classified as "Top Secret."**[146]

1985—US Air Force General George Havens, when he saw the recreation of the Ark that George Hagopian described, he said, **"We've seen that. We have photos of that. Our pilots have photographed that very object. It looks just like that. It is on a ledge. In fact, I was shown two slides of this object at Fort Leavenworth in a presentation for people assigned to Turkey."**[147]

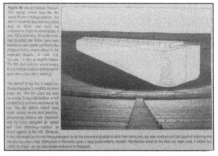

Walt Brown, "In the Beginning : Compelling Evidence for Creation and the Flood", 8th edition, Center for Scientific Creation, 2008, Figure 40.

---

[143] Balsiger and Seller, *Miraculous Messages from Noah's Flood to the End Times*, 221–226.

[144] Corbin, *The Explorers of Ararat and The Search for Noah's Ark*, 395–398.

[145] Corbin, *The Explorers of Ararat and The Search for Noah's Ark*, 408–409.

[146] Corbin, *The Explorers of Ararat and The Search for Noah's Ark*, 450–451.

[147] Corbin, *The Explorers of Ararat and The Search for Noah's Ark*, 458–459.

APPENDIX D

Quotes by Charles Darwin

Author of *The Origin of Species*

The following quotes are strong statements from Charles Darwin that the theory of evolution is neither scientific nor based on fact:

"Why then is not every geological formation and every stratum full of such intermediate links? Geology assuredly does not reveal any such finely graduated organic chain; and, this perhaps, is the most obvious and serious objection which can be urged against the theory."[148]

(Charles Darwin, "On the imperfection of the geological record," Chapter X, "The Origin of Species)

"For I am well aware that scarcely a single point is discussed in this volume on which facts cannot be adduced, often apparently leading to conclusions directly opposite to those at which I arrived. A fair result can be obtained only by fully stating and balancing the

---

[148] Charles Darwin, *The Origin of Species* (London: J.M. Dent & Sons Ltd., 1971), 292-293.

facts and arguments on both sides of each question; and this is here impossible."[149]

"You will be greatly disappointed (by the forthcoming book); it will be grievously too hypothetical. It will very likely be of no other service than collocating some facts; though I myself think I see my way approximately on the origin of the species. But, alas, how frequent, how almost universal it is in an author to persuade himself of the truth of his own dogmas."

(Charles Darwin, 1858, in a letter to a colleague on his "Origin of Species." As quoted in "John Lofton's Journal")[150]

"I was a young man with unformed ideas. I threw out queries, suggestions, wondering all the time over everything; and to my astonishment the ideas took like wildfire. **People made a religion of them.***"* [151]

"The fact of evolution is the backbone of biology, and biology is thus in the peculiar position of being a science founded on an unproved theory—is it then a science or a faith? Belief in the theory of evolution is thus exactly parallel to the belief in special creation—both are concepts which believers know to be true but neither, up to the present, has been capable of proof." [152]

"Christ Jesus and His salvation. Is not that the best theme?" [153]

---

[149] William J. Federer, *America's God and Country: Encyclopedia of Quotations* (New York: FAME Publishing, 1994), 198-199.

[150] "John Lofton's Journal," *The Washington Times*, February 8, 1984.

[151] Federer, *America's God and Country*, 198-199.

[152] L. Harrrison Matthews, FRS, *Introduction to Darwin's "The Origin of Species"* (London: J. M. Dent & Sons Ltd., 1971), xi.

[153] Federer, *America's God and Country*, 198-199.

APPENDIX E

QUOTES BY ALBERT EINSTEIN

FOUNDER OF THE THEORY OF RELATIVITY

"I have never found a better expression than 'religious' for this trust in the rational nature of reality and of its peculiar accessibility to the human mind. Where this trust is lacking science degenerates into an uninspired procedure. Let the devil care if the priests make capital of this. There is no remedy for that."[154]

"My religiosity consists of a humble admiration of the infinitely superior spirit who reveals himself in the slight details we are able to perceive with our frail and feeble minds. That deeply emotional conviction of the presence of a superior reasoning power, which is revealed in the incomprehensible universe, forms my idea of God."[155]

---

[154] Albert Einstein, *Lettres a Maurice Solovine reproduits en facsimile et traduits en francais* (Gauthier-Villars, 1956), 102-103.

[155] Albert Einstein, *The Quotable Einstein,* Edited by Alice Calaprice (Princeton, NJ: Princeton University Press, 2005), 195-196.

"I want to know how God created this world ... I want to know His thoughts; the rest are details." [156]

"We are in the position of a little child entering a huge library filled with books in many languages. The child knows someone must have written those books. It does not know how. It does not understand the languages in which they are written. The child dimly suspects a mysterious order in the arrangement of the books but doesn't know what it is. That, it seems to me, is the attitude of even the most intelligent human being to God. We see the universe marvelously arranged and obeying certain laws but only dimly understand those laws. Our limited minds grasp the mysterious force that moves the constellations."

– Max Jammer (a good friend of Albert Einstein)[157]

"Every one who is seriously engaged in the pursuit of science becomes convinced that the laws of nature manifest the existence of a spirit vastly superior to that of men, and one in the face of which we with our modest powers must feel humble."[158]

---

[156] Timothy Ferris, *Coming of Age in the Milky Way* (New York: Morrow, 1988), 177.

[157] Max Jammer, *Einstein and Religion* (Princeton, NJ: Princeton University Press, 1999), 48.

[158] Jammer, *Einstein and Religion*, 93.

ANOTHER REASON WHY WE SHOULD GET INVOLVED

Radio host Michael Knowles said on "Fox & Friends" that Democratic Socialists are urging Socialists to become teachers because they can't win a "fair fight."

A pamphlet by the Young Democratic Socialists of America, in conjunction with the Democratic Socialist Labor Commission, outlines a push for socialists to "take jobs as teachers" as a way to move teachers unions "in a more militant and democratic direction."

"They can't win a battle of ideas," he said.

He said that instead, Democratic Socialists are trying to cut off any thought of freedom by students and replace it with socialist ideology.[159]

---

[159] Fox News Insider, "Knowles: Dem Socialists Pushing to Infiltrate Schools Because 'They Can't Win in the Battle of Ideas," Fox News, August 25, 2018, http://insider. foxnews.com/2018/08/25/young-democratic-socialists-america-releases-pamphlet-targeting-teachers-unions-michael.

APPENDIX G

CREATIONIST ORGANIZATIONS IN THE UNITED STATES OF AMERICA[160]

Organization Name	Website	State
4th Day Alliance (ID)	www.4thdayalliance.com	CA
Access Research Network (CO)	www.arn.org/	CO
Akron Fossils & Science Center (OH)	www.akronfossils.com	OH
Alpha Omega Institute (CO)	www.discovercreation.org/	CO
American Portrait Films (OH)	www.theapologeticsgroup.com	OH
Answers In Genesis and The Creation Museum (KY)	www.answersingenesis.org/	KY
Antelope Valley Creation Science Museum (CA)	www.avcsa.org/	CA
Apologetics Press (AL)	www.apologeticspress.org	AL
Arizona Origin Science Association (AZ)	www.azosa.org/	AZ
Associates for Biblical Research (PA)	www.biblearchaeology.org	PA
Bible and Science Ministries (WA)	hoyle.nwcreation.net/	WA
Bible-Science Guy (Dr. William T. Pelletier)	bibliescienceguy.wordpress.com	

---

[160] Creation Ministries International, "Creationist organizations in the United States of America," accessed November 8, 2018, https://creation.com/creationist-organizations-in-the-usa.

Bible-Science Association of San Fernando Valley (CA)	www.bsa-ca.org/	CA
Biblical Discipleship Ministries (TX)	www.biblicaldiscipleship.org/	TX
California Institute of Omniology (CA)	www.omniology.com/	CA
Canyon Ministries (AZ)	www.CanyonMinistries.com	AZ
Center for Origins Research and Education (OR)	www.originsresearch.org/	OR
Center for Theology and Natural Resources (CA)	www.ctns.org/	CA
Christworks Ministries (VA)	www.cwm4him.org/	VA
Compass.org—Pointing to Christ (ID)	www.compass.org/	ID
Creation Adventures (Dr. Steve Austin)	creationadventures.com	PA
Creation Adventures Museum (FL)	www.sixdaycreation.com	FL
Creation Association of Puget Sound (WA)	caps.nwcreation.net/	WA
Creation Astronomy|Spike Psarris	www.creationastronomy.com/	
Creation Concepts (IL)	www.creationconcepts.org	IL
Creation Connection (MO)	www.gennet.org/mac/ mac.html	MO
Creation Dinosaurs and the Flood (NC)	www.sixdaycreation.com	NC
Creation Education Association (WI)	creationed.com/blogs	WI
Creation Education Center (WI)	www.cecwisc.org	WI
Creation Education Materials (TX)	www.creationanswers.net/ resources/dfwactiv.htm	TX
Creation Education Ministries (OR)	nwcreation.net/.net/	OR
Creation Engineering Concepts (OR)	www.creationengineering concepts.org/	OR
Creation Evolution Headlines (CEH: David Coppedge)	crev.info	
Creation Family Ministries (NC)	www.creationfamilyministries.org	NC
Creation Illustrated Magazine (CA)	www.creationillustrated.com	CA
Creation Instructional Association (NE)	www.creationinstruction.org/ index.php	NE
Creation Ministries International (GA)	creation.com	GA
Creation Moments, Inc. (MN)	www.creationmoments.com/	MN
Creation Museum of the Ozarks (MO)	www.creationmuseumoto.org/	MO
Creation Research of the North Coast (CA)	www.creationnews.org/	CA

Creation Research Science Educ. Fdn., Inc. (CRSEF) (OH)	www.worldbydesign.org	OH
Creation Research Society	www.creationresearch.org	
Creation Resource Foundation (CA)	www.creationresource.org	CA
Creation Safaris (CA)	www.creationsafaris.com	CA
Creation Science Association for Mid-America (MO)	www.csama.org/	MO
Creation Science Association of Central Illinois (IL)	www.gennet.org/mac/mac.html	IL
Creation Science Club of NJ	emporium.turnpike.net/C/cs/index.html	NJ
Creation Science Defense (GA)	www.creationdefense.org/	GA
Creation Science Evangelism (FL)	www.drdino.com/	FL
Creation Science Fellowship Inc. (PA)	www.csfpittsburgh.org/	PA
Creation Science Fellowship NM	www.creationsciencenm.org/	NM
Creation Science Network (WA)	www.creationproof.com/index.html	WA
Creation Science Research Center (CA)	www.parentcompany.com/csrc/	CA
Creation Science Society of Milwaukee (WI)	www.cssmwi.org/	WI
Creation Studies Institute (FL)	www.creationstudies.org/	FL
Creation Study Group of New Jersey (NJ)	www.csgnj.org/	NJ
Creation Study Group (SC)	www.creationstudygroup.org	SC
Creation Summit	creationsummit.com	OK
Creation Super Library	www.christiananswers.net/creation/	AZ
Creation Training Initiative	www.creationtraining.org/	ID
Creation Truth Foundation (OK)	www.creationtruth.com/	OK
Creation Worldview Ministries (FL)	www.creationworldview.org/	FL
Creationism.org (IN)	www.creationism.org/	IN
Crying Rocks Ministry (AZ)	www.cryingrocks.org	AZ
Dave's Creation Resources (IL)	www.davescreationresources.com/	IL
David Rives Ministries	davidrivesministries.org	TN
Defending the Christian Faith (Dr. John Leslie)	www.defendingthechristianfaith.org	
Design Science Association (OR)	pdxdsa.org	OR
Earth History Research Center (TX)	origins.swau.edu	TX

Earth Science Associates (TN)	www.halos.com/	TN
East Tennesse Creation Science Association (TN)	www.etcsa.org/	TN
Eden Communications/Films for Christ (AZ)	www.christiananswers.net/eden/ home.html=	AZ
Evolution Facts, Inc. (TN)	www.evolution-facts.org	TN
Evolution, a Fairytale for Grownups (Fred Williams)(CO)	www.evolutionfairytale.com	CO
Foundations in Genesis Idaho (ID)	www.figionline.com/	ID
Geoscience Research Institute (CA)	www.grisda.org/	CA
Greater Houston Creation Association (TX)	ghcaonline.com/	TX
His Creation (CO)	www.hiscreation.com/	CO
Indiana Creation Science Association (IN)	www.indianacreationscience.org	IN
Institute for Creation Research (TX)	www.icr.org/	TX
Institute for Scientific & Biblical Research (PA)	www.isbrministries.org	PA
Intelligent Design and Evolution Awareness Center (CA)	www.ideacenter.org/	CA
Intelligent Design Network–New Mexico (NM)	www.nmidnet.org/	NM
Intelligent Design Network, Inc. (KS)	www.intelligentdesignnetwork.org/	KS
Logos Research Associates (CA)	logosresearchassociates.org/	CA
Lutheran Science Institute (WI)	www.lutheranscience.org	WI
Master's International School of Divinity (IN)	www.mdivs.edu	IN
Media Angels (FL)	www.mediaangels.com	FL
Metroplex Institute for Origins Science (TX)	www.creationanswers.net/ resources/dfwactiv.htm	TX
Mid-Missouri Chapter of M.A.C. (MO)	www.gennet.org/mac/mac.html	MO
Midwest Creation Fellowship (IL)	www.midwestcreationfellowship.org	IL
Missouri Association for Creation (MO)	www.gennet.org/	MO
Molecular History Research Center	www.mhrc.net/	
Norm's Place (IN)	normsplace.homestead.com/ creation.html	IN
Northwest Creation Network (WA)	nwcreation.net/index.html	WA
Origin Science Association (VA)	http://vaosa.org	VA

Origins Resource Association (LA)	www.originsresource.org/	LA
Project Creation (TN)	www.projectcreation.org	TN
Reasons for Faith Ministries (OR)	kindell.nwcreation.net/	OR
Revealing Evidence of Creation (FL)	www.catiefrates.com/	FL
Revolution Against Evolution (MI)	www.rae.org//	MI
Rocky Mountain Creation Fellowship (CO)	www.youngearth.org/	CO
San Antonio Bible Based Science Association (SABBSA) (TX)	www.sabbsa.org	TX
Science Against Evolution (CA)	www.scienceagainstevolution.org/	CA
Science Partners (FL)	www.sciencepartners.net/	FL
Search for the Truth Ministries (MI)	searchforthetruth.net/	MI
South Bay Creation Science Association (CA)	www.creationinthecrossfire.com/	CA
The ARK Foundation of Daytona (OH)	www.arky.org/	OH
The Biblical and American Archaeologist (CA)	www.drfalesbaa.com	CA
The Insect Man (WV)	www.insectman.us	WV
The Life Science Prize	www.lifescienceprize.org	
The Monkey Trial	www.themonkeytrial.com	
The Sourcebook Project (MD)	www.science-frontiers.com	MD
The True Origin Archive (TX)	www.trueorigin.org/	TX
The Young Earth Creation Club (OH)	www.creationists.org/	OH
Triangle Association for the Science of Creation (NC)	www.tasc-creationscience.org/	NC
Tri-County Association for Creation (MO)	www.gennet.org/mac/mac.html	MO
Truth and Science Institute (OH)	www.havinganswer.net	OH
Twin Cities Creation Science Association (MN)	www.tccsa.tc/	MN
Understand The Times (CA)	www.understandthetimes.org	CA
Van Andel Creation Research Center (AZ)	www.creationresearch.org/ vacrc.html	AZ
www.creationism.org (IN)	www.creationism.org	IN
X-Evolutionist.com (OK)	www.x-evolutionist.com	OK

Discovery Institute's 'Academic Freedom Petition'

The Discovery Institute is asking folks to stand up for free speech on evolution by joining the more than 20,000 people (so far) who have signed their Academic Freedom Petition. Wherever academic freedom to question Darwin's theory is challenged, Discovery Institute may deliver this petition to government or educational officials to show the widespread support that exists for full discussion about Darwinian evolution.

(To sign the petition go to the site; https://freescience.today/petition/)

THE ACADEMIC FREEDOM PETITION[161]

We, the undersigned American citizens, urge the adoption of policies by our nation's academic institutions to ensure teacher and student academic freedom to discuss the scientific strengths and weaknesses of Darwinian evolution. **Teachers** should be

---

[161] Discovery Institute, "The Academic Freedom Petition," Free Science Today, accessed November 8, 2018, https://freescience.today/petition/.

protected from being fired, harassed, intimidated, or discriminated against for objectively presenting the scientific strengths and weaknesses of Darwinian theory. **Students** should be protected from being harassed, intimidated, or discriminated against for expressing their views about the scientific strengths and weaknesses of Darwinian theory in an appropriate manner.

Per the Discovery Institute,[162] when you sign the Academic Freedom Petition, you will get access to the following **free** resources:

1. A 57-page report on the top scientific problems with chemical and biological evolution.
2. A legal analysis of why academic freedom laws are constitutional.
3. Information on legislation you can propose in your state to support academic freedom on evolution.
4. Resources to promote academic freedom in your local school district.
5. A monthly **Academic Freedom Update** e-newsletter to keep you informed about debates over evolution and intelligent design around the nation.

Also, from Discovery Institute:[163]

Learn: Stories, Principles, History, Public Opinion, and Censor of the Year

Act: Sign the Petition, Start a Chapter, Celebrate Academic Freedom Day and Legislation

---

[162] Discovery Institute Seattle, WA 206-292-0401 www.discovery.org

[163] Other petitions by Discovery Institute—https://freescience.today/petition/.

BIBLIOGRAPHY AND RECOMMENDED READING

*T*here has been a lot of ink spilled recently making the case for the Biblical Creation. Just a few of the books in my possession are shown below:

- Ackerman, Dr. Paul and Bob Williams. *Kansas Tornado: The 1999 Science Curriculum Standards Battle.* Dallas: Institute for Creation Research, 1999.
- Batten, Don, Ken Ham, Jonathan Sarfati, and Carl Wieland. *The Revised & Expanded Answers Book: The 20 Most-Asked Questions About Creation, Evolution, & Book of Genesis Answered! Revised & Expanded Edition.* Green Forest, AR: Master Books, 1990.
- Behe, Michael J. *Darwin's Black Box: The Biochemical Challenge to Evolution.* New York: Free Press, 2006.
- Bergman, Jerry. *Slaughter of the Dissidents.* Southworth, WA: Leafcutter Press, 2008.
- Boice, James Montgomery. *Genesis, Volume 1: Creation and Fall (Genesis 1-11).* Grand Rapids: Baker Books, 1998.

- Brown, Michelle P. *In the Beginning: Bibles Before the Year 1000.* Washington, DC: Smithsonian Institution, 2006.
- Brown, Walt. *In the Beginning, Compelling Evidence for Creation and the Flood, 8th Edition.* Phoenix: Center for Scientific Creation, 2008.
- Cabal, Ted (ed.), et al. *The Apologetics Study Bible.* Nashville: Holman Bible Publishers, 2017.
- Clark, W.E. Le Gros. *The Antecedents of Man.* New York: Quadrangle Books, 1960.
- Clark, W.E. Le Gros. *The Fossil Evidence for Human Evolution.* Chicago: The University of Chicago Press, 1969.
- Coffin, Harold GG. And Robert H. Brown. *Origin by Design.* Hargestown, MD: Review and Herald Publishing, 2005.
- Colon, S.L. *The Serpent Within the Beast: Unveiling Satan as Evolution's Missing Link.* Meadville, PA: Christian Faith Publishing, 2017.
- Colson, Charles W. *A Dance with Deception.* Nashville: Word Publishing, 2004.
- Coppedge, James F. *Evolution: Possible or Impossible?* Grand Rapids: Zondervan, 1973.
- Darwin, Charles. *The Origin of Species.* London: J.M. Dent & Sons Ltd., 1971.
- Denton, Michael. *Evolution: A Theory in Crisis.* Chevy Chase, MD: Adler & Adler, 1986.
- Dowley, Tim (ed.) et al. *Eerdman's Handbook to the History of Christianity.* Carmet, NY: Guideposts, 1977.
- Epp, Theodore H. *The God of Creation.* Lincoln, NE: Back to the Bible Publications, 1972.
- Faulkner, Danny. *Universe by Design.* Green Forest, AR: Master Books, 2004.
- Feder, Kenneth L. *Encyclopedia of Dubious Archaeology.* Santa Barbara, CA: Greenwood, 2010.

- Ferrell, Vance. *The Evolution Handbook*. Altamonth, TN: Evolution Facts, 2002.
- Flew, Antony, *There Is A God: How the World's Most Notorious Atheist Changed His Mind*. New York: Harper One, 2007.
- Fortey, Richard. *Life: A Natural History of the First Four Billion Years of Life on Earth*. New York: Vintage Books, 1997.
- Geisler, Norman L. *Baker Encyclopedia of Christian Apologetics*. Grand Rapids: Baker Academic, 1998.
- Gish, Duane T., *Evolution: the Challenge of the Fossil Record*. Creation-Life Publishers, 1986.
- Gorney, Gazegorz and Janusz Rosikon. *Fatima Mysteries: Mary's Message to the Modern Age*. San Francisco: Ignatius Press, 2017.
- Ham, Ken. *Genesis and the Decay of the Nations*. Green Forest, AZ: Master Books, 1996.
- Ham, Ken. *The New Answers Book 1*. Green Forest, AR: Master Books, 2006.
- Ham, Ken. *The New Answers Book 2*. Green Forest, AR: Master Books, 2008.
- Hawking, Stephen and Leonard Mlodinow. *The Grand Design*, New York: Bantam Books, 2010.
- Hawkins, Gerald S. *Mindsteps to the Cosmos, 1st Edition*. New York: HarperCollins, 1983.
- Hodge, Bodie and Brian Osborne. *Quick Answers to Tough Questions*. Green Forest, AZ: Master Books, 2017.
- Huxley, Julian. *Religion without Revelation,* A Mentor Book, second edition, 1957.
- Institute for Creation Research, *Acts & Facts, Creation Basics,* 2013, Institute for Creation Research, Dallas, TX
- Institute for Creation Research, *Creation Basics & Beyond,* 2013, Institute for Creation Research, Dallas, TX
- Institute for Creation Research, *Guide to Creation,* 2013, Harvest House Publishers, Eugene, OR

- Jeanson, Nathaniel T. *Replacing Darwin: The New Origin of Species*. Green Forest, AZ: Master Books, 2017.
- LaHaye, Tim. *The Battle for the Mind, 1ˢᵗ Edition*. Old Tappan, NY: Fleming H. Revell Company, 1980.
- Levin, Harold L. *The Earth Through Time*. Edited by Ryan Flahive. Hoboken, NY: John Wiley & Sons, Inc., 2006.
- Livio, Mario. *Is God a Mathematician?* New York: Simon & Schuster, 2009.
- MacArthur, John. *The Battle for the Beginning: The Bible on Creation and the Fall of Adam*. Nashville: Thomas Nelson, 2001.
- McDowell, Josh. *Evidence That Demands a Verdict, Volume I*. Nashville: Thomas Nelson, 1979.
- Metaxas, Eric. *Miracles: What They Are, Why They Happen, and How They Can Change Your Life*. New York: Dutton Publishing, an imprint of Penguin Publishing Group, 2014. Used by permission.
- Midgley, Mary. *Evolution As A Religion*. New York: Routledge, 2002.
- Morris, Henry M. *Science and the Bible*. Chicago: Moody Publishers, 1986.
- Morris, Henry M. *The Genesis Record: A Scientific and Devotional Commentary on the Book of Beginnings*. Grand Rapids: Baker Book House, 1976.
- Morris, Henry M. *The Remarkable Record of Job*. Green Forest, AZ: Master Books, 1988/2000.
- Nelson, Vance, *Untold Secrets of Planet Earth: Flood Fossils*. Alberta, Canada: Untold Secrets of Planet Earth Publishing Company, 2014.
- Palmer, Douglas. *Prehistoric Past Revealed: The Four Billion Year History of Life on Earth*. Berkeley: University of California, 2006.
- Powell, Doug. *Guide to Christian Apologetics*. Nashville: Holman Reference, 2006.

- Ruse, Michael. *Darwinism As Religion: What Literature Tells Us about Evolution*. New York: Oxford University Press, 2016.
- Sanford, John C. *Genetic Entropy and the Mystery of the Genome Classroom Edition*. Massachusetts: Feed My Sheep Foundation, Inc., 2008.
- *Science Year, The World Book Science Annual—1966*, 1966, Field Enterprises Educational Corporation, Chicago, IL
- Sproul, R.C. and Keith Mathison. *Not A Chance: God, Science, and the Revolt Against Reason*. Ada Township, MI: Baker Books, 2014.
- Strobel, Lee. *The Case for a Creator*. Grand Rapids: Zondervan, 2004.
- Thomas, Brian. *Dinosaurs and the Bible*. Eugene, OR: Harvest House Publishers, 2015.
- Thomas, Cal. *Book Burning*. Wheaton, IL: Crossway, 1983.
- Thomas, R. Murray. *God in the Classroom: Religion and America's Public Schools*. Lanham, MD: R&L Education, 2008.
- Wells, Jonathan. *The Politically Incorrect Guide to Darwinism and Intelligent Design*. Washington, DC: Regnery Publishing, 2006.
- Whitcomb, John C. and Dr. Henry M. Morris. *The Genesis Flood: The Biblical Records and Its Scientific Implications*. Phillipsburg, NJ: Presbyterian & Reformed Publishing Co., 1961.
- Willmington, H.L. *Willmington's Guide to the Bible*. Fort Washington, PA: CLC Publications, 1984.
- Woetzel, Dave. *Chronicles of Dinosauria*. Green Forest, AZ: Masterbooks, 2013.
- Wysong, R.L. *The Creation-Evolution Controversy*. Midland, MI: Inquiry Press, 1991.

AFTERWORD

Let me let you in on a little secret. It is legal for Muslims to pray during school hours—and they do. It is also legal for Christians to pray during school hours—and they don't.

Pogo tells us:

Cal Thomas, in his book titled *Book Burning*, wrote:[164]

> *Our greatest enemy is the apathy of people of faith. We say we believe certain things. We memorize hundreds of Bible verses. We attend church three times a week. But we live as practical atheists.*
>
> *Do we write letters to the editor to express our viewpoints? Do we attend public school board meetings and voice our concerns?*
>
> *No, Secular Humanism isn't the ultimate enemy. We are. We could use a little less noise about the evil Secular Humanists and a lot more involvement by our own people in our own country.*

As our old comic strip friend Pogo once observed,

"We have met the enemy and he is US."

---

[164] Cal Thomas, *Book Burning* (Wheaton, IL: Crossway Books, 1983).

www.ingramcontent.com/pod-product-compliance
Ingram Content Group UK Ltd.
Pitfield, Milton Keynes, MK11 3LW, UK
UKHW031124120325
456135UK00006B/136